URBAN LANGUAGE SERIES

ROGER W. SHUY, GENERAL EDITOR

TEACHING STANDARD ENGLISH

IN THE INNER CITY

EDITED BY

RALPH W. FASOLD & ROGER W. SHUY

CENTER FOR APPLIED LINGUISTICS : 1970

ISBN: 87281-001-1

Library of Congress Catalog Card Number: 72-120748

Printed in the United States of America

Designed by Frank A. Rice

INTRODUCTION TO THE SERIES

The Urban Language Series is intended to make available the
results of recent sociolinguistic research concerned with the
position and role of language in a large metropolitan area.
The series includes descriptions of certain aspects of urban
language, particularly English, as well as theoretical consid-
erations relevant to such descriptions. The series also includes studies dealing with fieldwork techniques, matters of
pedagogy and relationships of urban language study to other
disciplines. Where appropriate and feasible, accompanying
tape recordings will be made available. Specifically excluded
from consideration are aspects of English as a second language
or second language learning in general.

It is hoped that the Urban Language Series will prove useful to several different kinds of readers. For the linguist,
the series will provide data for the study of language performance and for the development of linguistic theory. Historically, linguists have formulated theory from individual
rather than group performance. They have had to generalize
about what constitutes "standard" or "non-standard" from intu-
itive judgments or from very limited data. This series is
designed to make available large portions of language data as
well as analyses in order to broaden the knowledge from which
linguistic generalizations may come.

For the sociologist the series will provide access to
the nature of social stratification by means of language. It

is the contention of some scholars that a person's use of
language is one of the most important cues to his social
status, age, race or sex.

For the educator, the series will offer among other
things a description of·the very things which are most crucial to the classroom—the linguistic correlates which separate the accepted from the unaccepted.

Although the value of focussed attention on the special
problems of urban language has been recognized for some time,
relatively few substantial studies have been published. To
a certain degree, this series represents a pioneering venture
on the part of the Center for Applied Linguistics.

Roger W. Shuy
Director, Sociolinguistics Program
Center for Applied Linguistics

TEACHING STANDARD ENGLISH IN THE INNER CITY

PREFACE

Recently, there has been considerable interest in the non-standard dialects of disadvantaged children, especially disadvantaged Negro children. In spite of the interest, there has been relatively little discussion of the possible ways of dealing with nonstandard dialects. Currently, there are three approaches to the problem.

1. _Eradication_. In an editorial in the San Diego Union (September 10, 1969), Dr. Max Rafferty, State Superintendent of Public Instruction for the State of California, strongly urged the return to a pedagogical strategy of teaching that right is right and wrong is wrong with regard to the social varieties of American English:

> It is precisely education's job to deal in rights
> and wrongs. Because a child may count on his
> fingers and toes at home is no reason for his arith-
> metic teacher to let him keep doing it at school.
> And because a bigoted neighborhood may revel in
> racism doesn't make it okay for the civics instruc-
> tor to neglect teaching the Bill of Rights to young-
> sters who call that neighborhood home.
>
> Neither does the fact that mom and pop say "De cat
> has just split" when they mean "The man has just gone"
> make it right, any more than my Irish great-grand-
> father was permitted by his American teachers to go
> around voicing such Old Sod barbarisms as "Shure
> and begorra, 'tis a foine spaleen ye are, bad cess
> to ye."
>
> After his teachers had finished with him, great-
> grandad spoke good English, and he was thankful for
> it all his life. His parents went to their graves
> speaking brogue.

Although justifiable criticism may be made for selecting
this particular representation of the eradication position,
it nonetheless establishes the position very clearly.

A more scholarly position statement in support of eradication was made by Robert Green in reference to the more
generally held sympathy toward biloquialism noted at the 1964
Conference on Social Dialects and Language Learning:

> It was further indicated that if a person has a dia-
> lect that is peculiar to a given area and moves to
> another area, we should not attempt to change the
> dialect since it is acceptable in other parts of
> the United States. I would say that this point of
> view is not necessarily a defensible one, and I
> would again present the argument stressed pre-
> viously—that area dialects which allow one to be
> identified and discriminated against perhaps should
> be restructured.... The very inadequate speech that
> is used in the home is also used in the neighborhood,
> in the play group, and in the classroom. Since these
> poor English language patterns are reconstructed
> constantly by the associations that these young
> people have, the school has to play a strong role
> in bringing about a change in order that these young
> people can communicate more adequately in our society.
> (Robert Green, "Dialect Sampling and Language Values,"
> in R. Shuy (ed.) Social Dialects and Language Learning,
> Champaign, Ill., NCTE, 1965, pp. 122-123.)

It is not surprising that two leading educators such as
these men would adopt the eradication approach with respect
to the teaching of standard English to nonstandard speakers.
The English teaching profession has long nourished such a
position. Children are corrected in speech and writing from
their earliest days in the classroom to the last rites of
graduation. The anomoly of the situation is perhaps best
seen in the report of Murray Wax in his observations of how
English is being taught to the Pine Ridge Sioux Indians:

> Teachers are trained to criticize (the local dialect)
> as 'bad English,' and so, no sooner does the Indian
> child open his mouth to speak English, than he is
> branded publicly as speaking incorrectly. (Murray Wax,
> Rosalie Wax and Robert Dumont, "Formal Education in
> an American Indian Community," Social Problems, Spring,
> 1969, p. 82.)

If it seems undesirable to produce predictable regional
features such as those found among the Pine Ridge Sioux
Indians, how much more undesirable it must be to produce
socially identifiable features such as those found in ghetto
communities. The aim of English education, it then follows,
is to rid oneself of the stigma of those features by simply
eradicating the features.

2. Biloquialism. A second position is easier to describe
than to name. The term, functional bi-dialectalism was suggested at the Conference on Social Dialects and Language
Learning as a way of identifying a person's right to continue
speaking the dialect of his home (which may be nonstandard)
even after he has learned a standard school dialect. Since
the term dialect seems to carry such a heavy pejorative con-
notation these days, other terms have been suggested in place
of bi-dialectalism, including the recently coined term,
biloquialism. Whatever it is called, most linguists will
agree that a speaker of any language will make linguistic
adjustments to specific social situations. These adjustments
in phonology, grammar and lexicon will range anywhere from
the obvious adjustments between adults and small children to
the more complicated sociolinguistic switching between school,
home and playground talk. Those who encourage the adoption
of biloquialism feel that the teacher's job is not to eradicate playground English--or any other kind. Instead, teachers should help children to make the switch comfortably from
one setting to another.

3. Appreciation of Dialect Differences. Recently, a third
position has received some attention. There are a few linguists who have publicly advocated that, instead of offering
standard English to nonstandard speakers, we should not try
to change the speech of nonstandard dialect speakers at all.
If anything, we should attack the prejudices against non-
standard dialects which standard English speakers have. In

his review of the <u>Roberts English Series</u>, Wayne A. O'Neil
observes:

> Instead of "enriching" the lives of urban children
> by plugging them into a "second" dialect (... why
> don't we let everyone in for the fun and games;
> "enrich" the suburban kid with an urban dialect),
> we should be working to eradicate the language
> prejudice, the language mythology, that people grew
> into holding and believing. For there is clear
> evidence that the privileged use their false be-
> liefs about language to the disadvantage of the
> deprived. One way to stop this is to change non-
> standard speakers into standard dialect speakers
> at least for some of the time, i.e. when the non-
> standards are in the presence of the standards,
> currying favor of them, jobs from them, etc. This
> seems to me intolerable if not impossible. Another
> response to language differences would be to educate
> (especially the people in power) for tolerance of
> differences, for an understanding of differences.
> This could be naturally done, easily done in elemen-
> tary schools, but only by teachers who are them-
> selves free of language prejudice. In many ways
> this is the more important kind of language study
> that needs to be accomplished in the schools.
> (Wayne A. O'Neil, "Paul Roberts' Rules of Order:
> The Misuses of Linguistics in the Classroom", in
> <u>The Urban Review</u> II, no. 7.)

Those who share O'Neil's position argue that a brutal frontal
attack on the problem, such as the one advocated by those who
encourage the development of biloquialism, will be fruitless.
Arguing from this position, Thomas Kochman expresses his
lack of confidence in biloquialist techniques in an article
in a special anthology issue of <u>The Florida FL Reporter</u>
devoted to problems of language and culture for education:

> My second quarrel with such a program deals with what
> can be called its efficiency quotient. How much time
> and drill are required to acquire the new set of
> language habits necessary to produce even a mediocre
> and restrictive performance in standard dialect.
> Speech teachers tell me that with maximum cooperation
> it takes several months of drill to get a person to
> say <u>ask</u> to formerly said <u>aks</u>. My own observation
> tells me that the input in time and effort is pro-
> digious and the results negligible. (Thomas Kochman,
> "Social Factors in the Consideration of Teaching Standard
> English", in <u>The Florida FL Reporter</u> VII, no. 1, p. 87.)

It is further argued that this is not simply another case of
bonehead English, that a frontal attack will alienate non-
standard speakers from education, and that indirection is
likely to work better than a head-on attack since their
language will change of itself as they are introduced to a
wider and wider world. Furthermore, advocates of this position feel that it is as morally defensible to change the rest
of the world as it is to change the linguistic behavior of
the nonstandard spaker.

These three positions, then, characterize current thought
on the question of what to do about nonstandard English. It
will become obvious that the authors of the articles in this
volume have little sympathy with the eradication approach.
The premise that standard English is intrinsically better than
nonstandard dialects is explicitly rejected. Eradicationist
procedures have done little to improve the language of inner-
city children; on the contrary, such procedures have damaged
their self-confidence.

The third alternative, teaching respect for dialect differences, has much to recommend it. But there has been very
little discussion and no experimentation from this viewpoint.

The essays in the present volume are all written from
the second, or biloquialist perspective. Almost all biloquialist discussions of ways to deal with matters of language
in the education of inner-city Negro children have offered
only more-or-less programmatic suggestions of philosophies
and possible methodologies. The authors of the articles in
this volume attempt to go farther and to begin to answer the
questions of those who are prepared to accept the assumptions
and goals of the biloquialist position.

The article by William A. Stewart, a reprint of one of
the earliest articles on teaching standard English to speakers
of nonstandard dialects, compares the situation in American
cities to bilingual and near-bilingual situations elsewhere

in the world. The relationship between standard English and
the dialect of many inner-city Negroes shows striking similarities to problems in bilingual countries, a fact which may
come as a surprise to people who are used to thinking of non-
standard speech as merely sloppy or incorrect English.
Mr. Stewart argues that many of the techniques used to teach
foreign languages are applicable to the task of teaching
spoken standard English to inner-city Negro children. A
pioneer in the area of linguistic analysis of Negro dialects
and the author of numerous articles on the subject, Mr. Stewart
is now co-director of the Education Study Center, Washington,
D.C.

To a number of scholars in the fields of speech, education and psychology, the language of inner-city Negro children
is severely underdeveloped, showing the effects of an oppres-
sive social environment. As the previous article challenges
similar assumptions from the linguist's point of view, the
article by Joan C. Baratz serves as an introduction to the
educational issues involved in teaching standard English in
ghetto schools. The author also suggests a broad framework
for dealing with language problems in the inner-city. Mrs.
Baratz is co-director of the Education Study Center in Washington, D.C. She has published several articles on the speech
of inner-city Negro children in professional speech and education journals.

The first two articles argue that nonstandard Negro
dialects are not underdeveloped language, but are complete
grammatical systems related to standard English in somewhat
the same way that a foreign language is related to English.
If this is the case, it should be possible to describe the
grammar and pronunciation of Negro dialect and the rules which
govern it. The article by Ralph W. Fasold and Walt Wolfram is
an overview of some of the grammar and pronunciation features
of Negro dialect which are considered substandard by the general

public. Each of the authors has published several works on
Negro dialect and both are research associates at the Center
for Applied Linguistics.

Teachers who have to face the day-to-day problem of teaching English in inner-city schools will be less interested in
overviews and objectives than in more detailed descriptions
of the methods teachers can use in the classroom. Drawing on
considerable personal experience in teaching English to speakers of other languages and in teaching standard English to
inner-city children, Irwin Feigenbaum describes and illustrates this kind of methodology in his article. At the same
time, he deals with an issue which is frequently raised in
this connection -- whether or not nonstandard speech forms
should be used in the classroom. Mr. Feigenbaum is a project
linguist at the Center for Applied Linguistics and is the
author of English Now, a textbook for using the kind of techniques described and illustrated in his article.

With the linguistic features of nonstandard speech known
and a method for teaching alternatives available, it is still
important to have a systematic way to determine which features
are more crucial than others and therefore should be given
priority in a teaching program. Walt Wolfram, applying some
of the theoretical results of sociolinguistic research, has
developed principles for determining levels of cruciality.
Mr. Wolfram is the author of A Sociolinguistic Description of
Detroit Negro Speech (Urban Language Series, 5), and several
articles on related topics.

Many of the suggestions in this volume are new and somewhat controversial. The way of looking at nonstandard speech,
the details of the structure of the dialect involved, and the
methodology presented are all foreign to conventional teacher-
training programs. The article by Roger W. Shuy outlines ways
in which teacher-training should be overhauled in order to
adequately prepare teachers to deal with language in the

inner-city. Mr. Shuy is director of the Sociolinguistics
Program of the Center for Applied Linguistics. He has
authored a number of books and articles on dialectology and
applied linguistics.

   Teaching Standard English in the Inner City is an attempt
to take the next step toward practical solutions to these
language problems. If it ultimately contributes to improved
opportunities for at least some inner-city children, we shall
be well satisfied.

R.W.F.
R.W.S.
Washington, D.C.
1969

ACKNOWLEDGEMENTS

The editors are grateful to the Ford Foundation, the Carnegie Corporation of New York, and the United States Office of Education (Bureau of Research), for supporting the research upon which a number of the articles in this collection are based. Thanks are also due Allene Guss Grognet who provided invaluable editorial assistance, and Freda Ahearn who typed the manuscript for publication.

CONTENTS

FOREIGN LANGUAGE TEACHING METHODS IN
QUASI-FOREIGN LANGUAGE SITUATIONS

by William A. Stewart

If I were asked to indicate what I felt to be the most fundamental change which has taken place in the orientation of
language teaching in the United States during the past fifteen
or twenty years, I would point to the marked increase in realism evident in both the expressed purpose and the methodology
of language teaching. Of course, what I mean by "realism"
here is simply the view of language as it is rather than as
it ought to be, and of the learner's need for it as a personally useful tool of social interaction rather than as a
rotely learned device of principally esthetic value. Yet
this increase in realism has not been at the cost of a firm
basis in language teaching theory. On the contrary, language
teaching theory has been refined and enriched, not only through
its own considerable experience, but also by drawing heavily
from the knowledge which has been accumulating in linguistics,
psychology, sociology, and other behavioral sciences.

It is especially the first two of these -- linguistics
and psychology -- which have contributed most to the development of a number of basic theoretical assumptions about the
nature of language, the way it is learned, and the most suitable methods for teaching it. One of these I would like to
focus on, for it underlies the language teaching theme of this
paper; I am referring to the theoretical distinction between
"native" or "first" language teaching on the one hand, and
"foreign" or "second" language teaching on the other.

. . . .

Reprinted from William A. Stewart (ed.), Non-Standard Speech
and the Teaching of English (Washington, D.C., Center for
Applied Linguistics, 1964), pp. 1-15.

Insofar as language teaching in the school is concerned --
and I would like to restrict the scope of this paper to that
specific situation -- it is important to note that by school
age, that is, by the age of six or seven, the average, mentally
normal child will already have internalized most of the basic
phonological and grammatical patterns of at least one linguistic system (and indeed perhaps more, if the child has been
raised bilingually). The child will also have a fairly ready
command of a large number of lexical terms (less, however,
than an average adult) together with a surprising amount of
skill in their use or avoidance in terms of specific semantic
or social contexts.

Now, if the language being taught at school is essentially
the same as that already largely internalized by the child during the preschool language learning period, then it is clear
that language teaching in the school will be primarily concerned with giving the child a command of such supplemental
refinements as additional vocabulary, more complex or stylis-
tically restricted syntactical patterns, and of course reading
and writing skills. This, then, is "native" or "first" language teaching.

If, however, the language being taught at school is other
than the one in which the child has already acquired preschool
fluency (such as would be the case, say, in teaching Spanish
to a child previously monolingual in English, or English to a
Navaho monolingual -- or a Navaho-Spanish bilingual, for that
matter), then the teaching methods must of necessity be quite
different; the major task would be to impart a command of
precisely those kinds of basic linguistic patterns which were
already known in the native language teaching situation.
Furthermore, the fact that the new-language learner has already internalized the basic behavioral patterns of another
language -- patterns which differ from those to be learnt --
means that the language teaching techniques should take

special account of the ways in which the differences between
the native and the new languages are liable to produce interference problems for the learner. Language teaching of this
type is, of course, "foreign" or "second" language teaching.

This distinction between the two kinds of language teaching is fairly well known and accepted these days, but I have
felt it worth while to review it here, since for the remainder
of this paper I will be concentrating on extensions and modi-
fications of the methodological differences which it implies.

In the process of finding out about language behavior,
it sometimes happens that what has been generally accepted as
a more or less uniform whole turns out -- upon closer examination -- to be in reality a conglomerate of related but
empirically distinguishable linguistic systems. As is to be
expected, linguists are generally more aware of such divisions
than are language teachers, partly because linguists have a
more refined technique for dealing with minute differences in
language behavior, but also because the methodology of linguistic description is to start with discrete individual forms
of speech, and to build up from them generalizations about the
over-all pattern. Language teachers, on the other hand, have
been part of a tradition which has started with the assumption
of a more or less uniform whole, embodied, for example, in the
goal of teaching "the English language" or "the French language", and which takes only exceptional note of subvarieties
of speech. However, as I hope to illustrate, even for language teaching this generalized view of language as a uniform
whole is better left as a goal than taken as a starting assumption. Yet even linguists have on more than one occasion
found that the data, once collected, have necessitated a re-
vision of previously held views about a particular language.
An example of this would be the revised ideas about American
dialects which have resulted from the research carried out in
connection with the Linguistic Atlases of the United States.[1]

Perhaps a more striking example is furnished by the pidgins
and creoles spoken in various parts of the world, which were
once thought to be nothing more than "corrupted" forms of
certain European languages, but which subsequent analyses
have shown to represent fairly independent linguistic developments, and to constitute separate languages in their own
right.[2]

At this point, I am ready to illustrate how the linguistic characteristics of intra-language variation can have a
direct bearing on the language teaching methodology distinction I mentioned earlier. Let me begin with two cases which
are not really typical of the kind of situation usually found
in the United States, but which have the advantage of being
relatively well-defined from a linguistic point of view.

In Jamaica, standard English (based largely upon the
Southern British norm) is the official language of the island,
and the sole language of education. There is also a widely
used, unstandardized folk speech, referred to locally as "the
dialect". This designation is a purely sociolinguistic one,
in that it refers to the substandard nature of the folk speech,
rather than to its structural relation to standard English.
For the fact is that Jamaican "dialect" is popularly regarded
as nothing more than English badly spoken. Consequently, it
has been traditional in Jamaican schools to teach English to
country children much as it is taught to children in England --
in fact importing from there their textbooks and teaching
methods. These, needless to say, are with few exceptions
oriented toward first-language teaching, since most English
children are native speakers of the language.

Yet even the most energetic efforts at English teaching
in Jamaica characteristically meet with a general lack of
success which would be most unusual in England. The Jamaican
language teaching difficulties have been attributed to many
causes. Some, such as the low functional literacy level of

the island's population, probably are contributing factors.
However, it is now apparent to linguists that a major source
of the problem may lie in the fact that the Jamaican language
situation is different enough from that of England to require
a radically different approach. For Jamaican "dialect" is,
in its rural form at least, not linguistically a variety of
English at all, but is rather an English-based creole. That
is, it is an independent language with a large part of its
vocabulary derived historically from English, but with a grammar which is strikingly aberrant in many ways.[3] For example,
Jamaican Creole words like dem 'they, their, them', mi 'I,
my, me', fren 'friend', etc., sound quite like English,
though obviously substandard, as in:

dem a mi fren	'they are my friends'
mi a dem fren	'I am their friend'
mi a go si dem	'I am going to see them'

From the translations of fren occurring in the preceding
sentences, it will be noted that Jamaican Creole does not
indicate the pluralization of nouns where the number is apparent from the context (as it is, in the above cases, from
the number distinction implied in the subject pronouns dem
and mi). However, noun pluralization may be marked in cases
where the context leaves number ambiguous, and dem following
the noun is used for this purpose:

| mi a go si mi fren | 'I am going to see my friend' |
| mi a go si mi fren dem | 'I am going to see my friends' |

Thus it is apparent that there are several differences in
both the form and usage of pluralization in Jamaican Creole
and standard English; for the former, the marking of noun
pluralization is optional, but in the latter it is with few
exceptions, obligatory. Where the plural is marked in Creole,
it is done by the regular device of a free morpheme (structurally the same as the third person plural pronoun) following the noun. In English, pluralization is structurally

much more complex and often quite irregular. In addition,
the relation of Creole and English noun pluralization is
further complicated by the fact that the Creole uses a morpho-
logical plural for a purpose achieved in English by the use of
circumlocutions, e.g.:

    <u>mi fren-op Jien dem</u>   'I made friends with Jane and
                                   her crowd'

    A rural Jamaican, even after mastering all the complex
structural correlations between Creole and English noun
pluralization, would probably render the above Creole sentence
as "I made friends with Janes", which of course would mean
rather "I made friends with several girls named Jane" to the
native speaker of standard English.

    I think these examples -- and they could be duplicated
from almost all areas of Jamaican Creole and English structure -- furnish convincing evidence that the teaching of
standard English in rural Jamaica would benefit by a very
positive shift from a native language to a foreign language
teaching approach.

    In Liberia, where English is also the official language
(in this case, based largely upon American norms), children
are taught the standard language by traditional, native language methods, with heavy reliance upon texts imported from
the United States. Yet, even by the time they first enter
school, most Liberian children have acquired a fairly fluent
command of Liberian Pidgin English, which is widely spoken
in the streets of Monrovia, along the main communication
routes of the interior, by soldiers, and in inter-tribal
villages and markets.[4]

    There are a large number of structural differences be-
tween Liberian Pidgin English and standard English, and it
is interesting to note that for tribal Liberians the Pidgin
patterns seem to cause more interference problems in their
English than do the patterns of the African vernaculars which

they speak at home and actually learn first. A few examples
will serve to illustrate this kind of interference. Liberian
Pidgin English marks the present tense of verbs by adding
-in to the verb stem, e.g.:

    ah ronin[5]   'I am running'

The verb stem used alone indicates the past tense in the Pidgin, e.g.:

    ah ron   'I ran'

Because of this, Liberian children, when attempting to refer
in English to an event in the past, will often use the verb
stem alone, though of course this is actually the simple
present in English. The possibility of this latter function
for the verb stem in English does not occur to the Liberian
child, since the meaning of the English simple present is
expressed in Pidgin with le (pronounced [lέ]), e.g.:

    ah le ron   'I run'

General predication also causes problems, since Liberian
Pidgin English has three separate constructions where standard English always uses the verb to be:

    zero in noun adjective clauses:

        dey smoh   'they are little'

    biy in noun-noun clauses:

        i biy teybu   'it is a table'

and dey to indicate presence or position:

        shiy dey deh   'she is there'

These Pidgin patterns can often be seen to underlie mistakes Liberian school children make in attempting to produce
English equivalents. Although one would expect the Liberian
language situation to make it more appropriate to teach English as a foreign language than as a native language, it may
come as a surprise to many that the language most likely to
constitute the major source of interference is Liberian Pidgin English rather than any of the vernaculars.

Language situations similar to the Jamaican and Liberian
ones in that they involve pidgins and creoles which are related to the official standard exist in other parts of the
Caribbean and West Africa, as well as in certain parts of
Asia.[6]

Here in the United States, the only language teaching
situation involving an English-based creole that I am aware
of is that of teaching English to speakers of Gullah. But
the point of my Jamaican and Liberian examples was not solely
that English-based creole or pidgin speakers need to be taught
standard English as a foreign language (although I do maintain
that this is the case). Rather, I intended it as an illustration of the more general fact that there may be cases where
the structural relationship between standard English and
varieties of speech which are sociologically accepted as mere
substandard variants of it are in fact reminiscent of foreign
language relationships. An example which comes immediately
to mind concerns Mexican-American English.[7] Structurally, it
is more like Spanish than English in its phonology, but more
like English in its grammar and vocabulary, and in certain
ways it is also syncretic and innovating. For example, since
final consonant clusters of the type /-nt/ and /-nd/ do not
normally occur in the dialect, the standard colloquial English
contrast between <u>can</u> and <u>can't</u> is handled by a consistent
stress difference; compare:

/xì kàŋ gó#/   'he can go'
with
/xì káŋ gô#/   'he can't go'

Note that a stress differentiation of this type for verbs
is not a normal Spanish phenomenon, nor are some of the stress
sequences particularly English. A certain amount of the basic
structure of this dialect is clearly deviant from that of
standard English, and foreign language teaching methods ac-
cordingly seem appropriate to some degree in English teaching involving speakers of this dialect.

For my last illustration, I will turn to English teaching in another American dialect situation. Although it clearly has less of a real foreign language element than the preceding one, it nevertheless involves enough structural mismatch to warrant, if not a full foreign language teaching approach, then at least one which still takes sufficient account of the fact that conflicts between different linguistic structures underlie many of the learner's difficulties. This particular linguistic situation -- itself a by-product of fundamental changes which are taking place in the American social and economic order -- offers the teaching profession one of its greatest current challenges.

I am referring to the teaching of English in many of our large northern and west coast urban communities to speakers of various substandard dialects of English which have come there primarily through migration from the southern Atlantic and Gulf states. The fact that in most such communities the majority of these dialect speakers are Negroes means that the English teaching situation -- complex enough in terms of the linguistics alone -- is further complicated by the intrusion of social, cultural, economic, and even political factors.

In their native region, dialects of this type evolved within an over-all sociolinguistic framework in which they stood in a structurally close and socially well-defined relationship to local varieties of standard English. However, migration to the North and the West Coast has taken the dialects out of that setting and brought them into direct contact with varieties of English -- both standard and substandard -- which are often structurally very different, and into a new sociological environment where the intruding dialects are regarded with much less general indulgence than they were at home. The nongradient nature of the structural relationship between the immigrant dialects and the traditional ones in the northern communites tends to emphasize

the substandard nature of the imported speech forms and, in
cases where they are brought in and used primarily by Negroes,
dialectal traits often acquire associations with racial iden-
tity. This can happen even though such traits may have been
shared by white and Negro alike in their home territory, and
in spite of the fact that in the northern communities there
may be Negroes in whose speech such traits are totally absent.[8] No doubt in part because of this racial association
of imported dialect features in the new community, Negro
immigrants and their descendents may show a tendency to retain some of them. In fact, a fairly uniform in-group dialect may come into existence which, due to dialect mixing
and innovation, may come to be unique to that community, even
though other communities may be made up of essentially the
same immigrant composition. In most such communities, there
may be a further linguistic differentiation between immigrant
Negro and native-born Negro, with the latter's speech being
typically closer to the northern standard. But this is by no
means universal, since extremely heavy migration may cause
linguistic swamping, with the result that even native-born
persons may come to have the same type of speech as the immigrants.[9]

Although the actual linguistic details of such immigrant
dialect situations are currently being analyzed and described
in some communities, many others still remain unstudied, and
comparisons between the main characteristics of the dialect
situations in various communities have yet to be made.[10]
However, I can give a few examples of this type of language
teaching problem based on personal observations in Washington,
D.C. These examples may seem simple or obvious, but it is
precisely for that reason that I have chosen them as isolated
illustrations of what is really a vast complex of interrelated
linguistic and sociolinguistic problems.

Let me begin with a case of phonological mismatch. Among
the consonants used in virtually all varieties of standard
English, there is a paired series of consonants which can be
diagrammatically organized according to place and manner of
articulation as follows:

	Bilabial fricative	Apico-dental fricative	Apico-alveolar stop
Voiced	/v/	/ð/	/d/
Voiceless	/f/	/θ/	/t/

These all occur word initially, e.g.:

/vot/ vote   /ðɪs/ this   /du/ do
/fʊt/ foot   /θiŋ/ thing   /tu/ two

medially, e.g.:

/nɛvɚ/ never   /mʌðɚ/ mother   /lædɚ/ ladder
/sʌfɚ/ suffer /nʌθiŋ/ nothing /mætɚ/ matter

and finally, e.g.:

/lʌv/ love   /brið/ breathe /nid/ need
/tʌf/ tough   /brɛθ/ breath   /nit/ neat

In contrast, a diagram of the consonant phonemes covering essentially the same articulatory area for a common type
of substandard Washington English would be:

	Bilabial fricative	Apico-alveolar stop
Voiced	/v/	/d/
Voiceless	/f/	/t/

Note that in this dialect there are no apico-dental frica-
tives, standard English /ð/ and /θ/ showing up as /d/ and
/t/ in initial positions, and usually as /v/ and /f/ elsewhere. Thus the middle column of the word list previously
cited would appear, for this type of English, as follows:

/dɪs/ this
/tiŋ/ thing
/mʌvə/ mother
/nʌfɨn/ nothing
/briv/ breathe
/brɛf/ breath

Here, there are two teaching problems. First, the new
phonemes /ð/ and /θ/ must be taught, i.e. their articulation
as well as the recognition of their contrast both with /d/
and /t/ and with /v/ and /f/. Second, their occurrence in
specific words must be taught, so that /d/, /t/, /v/ and /f/
are replaced in the appropriate ones, but in no others. For
the first of these, the English teacher could profit from
foreign language teaching techniques devised for teaching
phonemic contrasts which are not in the native language of
the learners.[11]

In standard English, both the definite and indefinite
articles have two different pronunciations in unstressed
position, depending upon whether the following word begins
with a consonant phoneme (e.g. /bʊk/ book/ or a vowel phoneme (e.g. /ok/ oak). The variants are:

	Definite article	Indefinite article
Before a consonant phoneme	/ðə/	/ə/
Before a vowel phoneme	/ði/	/ən/

Thus most speakers of standard English say /ðə búk/ and
/ə búk/, but /ði ók/ and /ən ók/.

This kind of automatic alternation in the pronunciation
of the articles is incorporated into the orthography of the
indefinite article, where /ə/ is written as a and /ən/ as an,
e.g. a book, an oak, but it is not recognized for the definite
article, both pronunciations of which are written the, e.g.
the book, the oak.

In Washington substandard English, the articles are
commonly pronounced /ðə/ and /ə/ both before words beginning
with consonant phonemes, and those beginning with vowel phonemes. The only difference is that in the latter case the
vowel of the article and the initial vowel of the following
word are separated by a junctural phenomenon, usually a
glottal stop, e.g. [ðə ˀ ok], [ə ˀ ok].

Now, for the standard English speaker, the spelling difference a vs. an presents no problem, since he simply writes
what he says, while he can ignore his pronunciation differences for the definite article, since it has no orthographic
variation. For the non-standard speaker, however, the correct
selection of a or an in spelling the indefinite article may
cause problems, because the variation matches nothing in his
linguistic behavior.

In teaching the non-standard speaker the correct use of
a and an, acquainting him with the abstract phonological
rules (from a dialect which the learner does not speak) underlying the spelling variation would hardly seem to be either
a realistic or an enduring solution to the problem. Nor would
instruction based on purely orthographic rules, like "write a
before consonant letters and an before vowel letters", since,
even if understood, it could produce such unacceptable results as a honor and an use. Some purely orthographic differences can easily be handled by the simple device of
memorizing word lists, representing this or that spelling.
Such a solution is not feasible in this case, however, because the word lists dividing a from an would ultimately
include every noun and adjective in the English language.
It seems to me that the most direct and enduring solution to
this particular spelling problem is simply to get the non-
standard speaker to internalize the relevant phonological
behavior of the standard dialect, upon which the spelling
rules are based. This could be done using much the same kind
of pattern drills that are used for teaching English-speaking
learners of French such variations as /la/ vs. /l/.

A more complex problem of essentially the same sort is
encountered in the teaching of standard English verb usage
to non-standard speakers in the same dialect situation. Perhaps the most immediately apparent case of mismatch in this
area involves the absence with many speakers of the third

person singular marker -s on the present tense form of standard English verbs, e.g. substandard he know for standard he
knows.[12] Technically more serious, however, are cases where
mechanisms of predication and even the overall organization
of the verbal systems may be different in the two types of
speech. For example, certain kinds of predication without
a verb exist in substandard speech where standard English
uses the linking verb to be, e.g. substandard they tired and
she my sister beside standard they are tired and she is my
sister. An example of more general verbal system differences
is to be found in the dialect usage of some spakers who apparently have no inflectional contrast to match the preterite
vs. simple present of standard English. Thus a form like
he go will be used by such speakers where standard English
would use he went as well as where it would use he goes.
For this type of substandard dialect, the main distinction
is aspectual, being between non-durative (cf. the he go construction) and durative, e.g. he goin', this last construction being roughly equivalent to standard he is going or, in
some cases, he was going.[13]

I think that the foregoing examples are sufficient to
demonstrate that, for this dialect situation, verbal usage
is sometimes different from that of standard English. Furthermore, since the individual cases of mismatch may derive from
more general deviations in the over-all organization of the
two verbal systems themselves, it seems clear that isolated
"mistakes" will not necessarily be amenable to patchwork
correction. On the contrary, it would appear that the most
satisfactory approach to the teaching of standard verbal usage
would be of a type similar to one now being used in many of
the newer foreign language teaching materials. In these, the
corrective exercises are based upon a preliminary comparison
of the way in which the learner's verbal system agrees with
or differs from that of the language being taught.

In the four preceding English teaching case histories
which I have selected to illustrate the suitability of foreign
language teaching methods in what I have termed "quasi-foreign"
language situations, the actual structural distance between the
non-standard, English-like, pre-school speech of the learner
and the standard English being taught has varied from case to
case. In the Jamaican and Liberian situations, the non-
standard varieties were different enough from standard English to have prompted linguists to classify them as independent languages. In the American situations the difference
was less marked, although a certain amount of structural devi-
ation from standard English was still evident. From the language teaching point of view, what was common to all of these
cases was the fact that, in spite of striking structural
similarities in certain areas (such as in vocabulary), structural dissimilarities in other areas (such as in grammars)
have given rise to language learning problems of a type which
are similar to foreign language learning problems, and hence
render desirable the use of foreign language methods in English teaching.

With this conclusion established, it will be apparent
that the development of more suitable language teaching
materials for situations like the foregoing ones has to de-
pend heavily upon the availability of good linguistic descriptions of those non-standard varieties of speech which are
normally used by the learners of the language to be taught.
Of course, the linguist will want such forms of speech described anyway -- as additional samples of human language
behavior, if for no other reason.[14] However, the educator
or language teacher, who may be tempted to look down on non-
standard varieties of speech, should bear in mind that linguistic descriptions of them, far from being mere scholastic
curiosities, can serve as a very useful basis for more effective teaching of the kind of language which he or she is
deeply interested in getting the learner to use.

NOTES

1. See Allen, "The Linguistic Atlases: Our New Resource".
    Also compare the three dialect maps of the United States
    given as figures 3, 4, and 5 in Bronstein, The Pronunci-
    ation of American English, which represent major revisions
    in linguists' interpretations of the dialectal subdi-
    visions of American English. Incidentally, there has
    recently appeared an admirable interpretation for English
    teachers of the newer dialect data. This is Malmstrom
    and Ashley's Dialects -- U.S.A.

2. For an exemplary case history of one such pidgin language,
    see Hall, Hands Off Pidgin English!

3. By "grammar", I obviously mean the patterns of language
    structure rather than a set of rules in a book. This
    distinction between linguistic grammar and formal grammar
    is now widely known and accepted in the United States,
    but it is much less familiar to Jamaican language teach-
    ers. To most of them, Jamaican Creole "has no grammar",
    simply because its structural patterns have never been
    formally codified within the culture. For a linguistic
    description of Jamaican Creole, see Bailey's dissertation,
    "Jamaican Creole Syntax".

4. As is the case with Creole in Jamaica, Pidgin English has
    no independent sociolinguistic status in Liberia, and in-
    deed is known by no specific name. Where it is referred
    to at all, it tends to be called "colloquial English",
    "bad English", or, in Monrovia, "Water Street English".
    An important difference between the Jamaican and Liberian
    situations is that while Creole is the native -- and
    only -- language of most Jamaicans, Liberian Pidgin Eng-
    lish is usually a second language for tribal Liberians
    who are native speakers of an African vernacular such as
    Bassa or Kpelle. Incidentally, Liberian Pidgin English
    is structurally quite different from the Nigerian and
    Cameroun varieties of English-based Pidgin, which are
    closely related to Sierra Leone Krio.

5. This -in, pronounced [ĩ], is historically related to the
    standard English morpheme written -ing. The Liberian
    Pidgin English examples are given here in a tentative,
    quasi-phonemic spelling based on preliminary linguistic
    investigations which I carried out in Liberia under the
    auspices of Educational Services, Inc. and the Center for
    Applied Linguistics.

6. I am currently preparing, for the use of Educational Ser-
    vices, Inc. in West Africa, a language manual for primary

school teachers in countries where instruction is given
in English, but where an English-based pidgin or creole
is widely used outside the classroom. Its main purpose
is to inform the teacher about likely language interference problems, and techniques for avoiding or correct-
ing them. The manual is intended primarily for mathe-
matics teachers in Liberia and Sierra Leone, but it is
being written so as to also make it useful for teachers
of other subjects and in other areas with a similar language situation, such as Nigeria, the Cameroun, and the
British Caribbean. [Editor's Note: The above manual
was never completed. However see, Language Teaching,
Linguistics, and the Teaching of English in a Multi-
lingual Society, Kingston: University of the West Indies,
Faculty of Education, 1965, to which the author contributed.]

7. Here I do not refer to the kind of English which a mono-
    lingual Spanish speaker in Mexico may end up with after
    having taken English in school. Rather, I refer to a
    special dialect of American English spoken in the South-
    west by a considerable number of Americans of Mexican
    descent, who are usually bilingual in it and some variety
    of Mexican or Southwestern Spanish.

8. See Raven McDavid's articles, "Some Social Differences
    in Pronunciation" and "The Relationship of the Speech of
    American Negroes to the Speech of Whites".

9. This phenomenon is certainly common in Washington, D.C.,
    where it is easy to find cases involving second or third
    generation Washington Negro families in which the parents
    are speakers of a quite standard variety of English, but
    where the children's speech is much closer to that of the
    newer immigrants. The explanation seems to be that heavy
    post-war immigration has dialectally swamped much of the
    younger generation of native Washingtonians. This phe-
    nomenon, incidentally, seems to support the theory that
    children learn more language behavior from members of
    their own peer group than from their parents, and sug-
    gests that educator concern over the quality of "language
    in the home" may be misplaced.

10. Research projects for studying the sociolinguistic situ-
    ation -- including urban Negro speech -- are presently
    being carried out in Chicago, under the direction of
    Raven I. McDavid, Jr., and in New York City by William
    Labov of Columbia University. In Washington, D.C., a
    program for the study of the speech of school-age chil-
    dren, involving the cooperation of the Center for Applied
    Linguistics and the District of Columbia Public Schools,

is currently in the proposal stage. [Editor's Note: The
Washington, D.C. program, known as The Urban Language
Study, began in October 1965, and is still in operation
as part of CAL's Sociolinguistics Program.]

11. Many Washington speakers have /ð/ and /θ/ word-initially,
    with the standard distribution, but generally have /v/
    and /f/ medially and finally. For them, the teaching
    problem is essentially one of bringing about sound sub-
    stitutions in the appropriate places.

12. As far as the communication of meaning is concerned,
    this absence of verbal -s in substandard speech causes
    no ambiguity, since the relevant information is usually
    supplied by the noun or pronoun. Socially, however, its
    use is quite important, because the presence of verbal
    -s in the appropriate places appears to serve as one of
    the criteria distinguishing "educated" from "uneducated"
    speech. This is one of those many cases where, in con-
    tent, substandard English is just as expressive as
    standard English -- the two differing primarily in form.
    Yet is is on the basis of just such differences in lin-
    guistic form that social judgments regarding the speaker
    are often made.

13. Either fortuitously or because of a historical connec-
    tion of some sort, this same dominance of aspect over
    tense is found in certain Caribbean creole languages.

14. For an outstanding example of the kind of scientific
    description which can be made of substandard and
    socially deprecated varieties of speech, even where
    these may be subjugated to the norms of a closely re-
    lated but standardized dialect of high prestige, see
    Sievertsen's Cockney Phonology.

BIBLIOGRAPHY OF WORKS CITED

Allen, Harold B. "The Linguistic Atlases: Our New Resource",
    The English Journal 45.188-194 (1956). Also reprinted
    in the following item, pp. 212-219.

-----, ed. Readings in Applied English Linguistics. 2nd ed.
    New York, Appleton-Century-Crofts, Inc., 1964.

Bailey, Beryl L. "Jamaican Creole Syntax: A Transformational
    Approach". Unpublished Ph.D. Dissertation, Columbia
    University, 1964.

Bronstein, Arthur J. The Pronunciation of American English:
    An Introduction to Phonetics. New York, Appleton-Century-
    Crofts, Inc., 1960.

Hall, Robert A., Jr. Hands Off Pidgin English! Sydney,
    Australia, Pacific Publications Pty., Ltd., 1955.

Malmstrom, Jean and Annabel Ashley. Dialects -- U.S.A.
    Champaign, Illinois, National Council of Teachers of
    English, 1963.

McDavid, Raven I., Jr. "Some Social Differences in Pro-
    nunciation", Language Learning 4.102-116 (152-3).
    Also reprinted in Harold B. Allen, ed., Readings in
    Applied English Linguistics, pp. 251-261.

----- and Virginia Glenn McDavid. "The Relationship of the
    Speech of American Negroes to the Speech of Whites",
    American Speech 26.3-17 (1951).

Sievertsen, Eva. Cockney Phonology. Oslo, Norway, Oslo
    University Press, 1960.

EDUCATIONAL CONSIDERATIONS FOR TEACHING STANDARD ENGLISH TO NEGRO CHILDREN

by Joan C. Baratz

It is commonplace to observe that lower class Negro school children do not speak like white children -- lower or middle class. Although there is considerable agreement on this empirical observation, there is a great deal of discussion and debate concerning its source, significance and consequence.

The Difference-Deficit Question

The systematic research on the language of lower class Negro children has produced two general conceptual vantages concerning their verbal abilities -- one camp, composed generally of psychologists and educators, has tended to view the language of black children as defective -- i.e. the language of Negro children is underdeveloped or restricted in some way. These experimenters attribute the deficit to environmental factors, frequently observing that the mother doesn't interact with the child enough, doesn't read books to him, etc. The other camp, composed mainly of linguists, has viewed the language of lower class Negro children as a different yet highly structured, highly developed system.

For several years these two "camps" operated quite independently -- psychologists went along describing deficiencies while linguists went about detailing differences.

. . . .

Another version of this paper under the title of "Who Should Do What To Whom...and Why?" appeared in Linguistic-Cultural Differences and American Education, a special anthology issue of The Florida FL Reporter 7:1.75-77, 158-159 (1969).

Recently, however, with the advent of interdisciplinary programs, each group has developed an increased awareness of the
other's position.

The question then arises as to whether a deficit model
and a difference model can co-exist. Can a language be a
fully developed, complex system (according to the linguists)
and yet still be deficient -- insofar as it produces speakers
with language and cognitive deficits (according to certain
psychologists)? Or to put it another way, can these children
have speech and language problems that affect inter- and
intra- personal communication that are not related to the
dialect? Aside from about 5% of lower class Negro children
who along with 5% of the other populations of children, have
speech and language deficits due to neuro-physiological or
psychological difficulties, it is not possible to generally
characterize the speech of lower class children as deficient.

Those psychologists who wish to believe that there is
such a thing as a fully developed different system that produces cognitive deficiency rely heavily on the writings of
Basil Bernstein, while not always showing that they clearly
understand his work. Bernstein speaks of the language of
lower class speakers as a "restricted code" as opposed to the
"elaborated code" available to the middle class. For Bernstein, this distinction seems to refer to language use, with
no clear indication that speakers limited to restricted code
suffer any cognitive deficit; only that their orientation
toward the verbal channel will be different from that of
elaborated code speakers.[1] Many followers of Bernstein,
however, have confused superficial forms with specific processes. If a form is missing in Negro non-standard, it is
assumed that the process is absent as well. To show the fallacy of this, one need only point out that in Negro non-
standard the conceptual scheme "if" is, under certain conditions, used without any overt representation of the form

"if". Thus while in standard English one might say "I don't
know if Robert can come over tonight", in Negro non-standard
the equivalent would be "I don't know can Robert come over
tonight." In the standard English version a vocabulary item
is used to fulfill the interrogative function; in Negro non-
standard a structural shift is used. Nevertheless, both
sentences (standard English and Negro non-standard) are
equally capable of conveying the questionableness of Robert's
availability in the evening.

The researchers who concerned themselves with applying
the restricted and elaborated code thesis to explanations of
cognitive impairment in young black children not only relied
heavily on superficial structural differences in language
production (whose relationship to cognition is not clear),
but also these same researchers failed to deal with the socio-
cultural variable and the role it might play in speech elicitation. For example, the task, "describe this picture", may
be perceived differently by different groups in different
settings. Mexican peasants, when given a picture of people
engaged in an activity, are likely to "describe the picture"
by detailing personality factors "she's sad", whereas lower
class English boys may be more likely to describe the action
that the individuals are engaged in -- "he's throwing him the
ball." Middle class white Americans may feel that "to describe a picture" is to elaborate on all the details of a
picture -- i.e. setting, action and feelings. This does not
mean, of course, that Mexican peasants are incapable of res-
ponding to pictures by detailing the setting or the actions
that are taking place. One need only define the task as
such, i.e. "tell me what is happening in this picture",
rather than "describe the picture."

Erickson[2] has illustrated that black children use both
restricted and elaborated codes -- the frequency of either
code being determined by the subject matter, the setting,

and to whom the individual is speaking. He has demonstrated the futility of presuming that black children do not use elaborated codes.

Perhaps of more importance than the demonstration that black children use both elaborated and restricted codes is the evidence most clearly demonstrated by Labov that one can produce highly abstract concepts while using extremely "restricted" codes.

A black teenager was asked, "Just suppose there is a God; would he be white or black?" When he responded "He'd be white" the interviewer asked "Why?" "Why? I'll tell you why. Cause the average whitey out here got everything, you dig? And the nigger ain't got shit, y'know y'unerstan'? So-um-for-in order for that to happen, you know it ain't no black God that's doin' that bullshit." The code the teen-ager has used is clearly non-standard and, in terms of the Bernstein classification system, can be viewed as "restricted". Nonetheless in terms of logic and complexity it is no less restricted than the elaborated standard English equivalent "I know that God isn't black, because if he were, he wouldn't have arranged the world the way it is."[3]

Those researchers who would feel that language styles can be hierarchically distributed with more elaborated codes indicating more complex thought will first have to deal with the matter of equivalences across codes. The absence of such discussions in the literature, along with the fact that there has been little demonstration that the presence of certain linguistic forms and usages impair cognitive ability makes it quite clear that the deficit model cannot be applied in re-lation to cognitive ability and language style.

Indeed, the fact that the language structure and style is different in the black community from that of the white mainstream serves only to indicate that the tests that black children are given initially cannot be used as measurements

of potential so much as evidence of what black children know
about the mainstream culture. Their poor performance by
white mainstream standards merely indicates that they must be
taught how to negotiate in a cultural setting that is different from their own.

Nonetheless, the differences in language structure and
usage can be handicapping to the non-standard speaker when he
is expected to operate in a system that demands the use of
standard English structure and style. This language difference will create a problem in terms of oral communication in
standard English settings. But the scope is even broader.
His success in school programs may be hindered because interference from his different linguistic system can cause difficulties in his learning to read and write standard English,
the lingua franca of the public schools.

Is it Necessary for Black Children to Learn Standard English?

Given the fact that many black children do not speak
standard English upon entering school (and quite frequently
still do not speak it when leaving school), the question is
raised: what should the school system do about this situation?
Should the school system require that these children learn
standard English?

There are those voices in the academic community who say
no, standard English need not be taught to these children.[4]
These critics rightly feel that the child's language system
is a fully developed, totally adequate linguistic system
which is no better or worse than standard English and therefore, they think, it should be accepted as a perfectly adequate substitute for standard English.

Nevertheless, there are several discrepancies, overt and
implied, in the argument against teaching standard English to
black children. First, although it is true from a linguistic
viewpoint that all dialects (Negro non-standard, Standard
American English, Oxford English, etc.) are equal, it is also

true from a social viewpoint that some dialects are considered more valuable than others in certain contexts. The linguistic relativity, then, does not take into account the social reality. Middle class individuals still rate Standard American English as more desirable than Negro speech. Pejorative ratings are associated with Negro non-standard speech despite its viability, complexity and communicativeness as a linguistic system.[5]

Indeed, despite the fact that various dialects may be used orally, the exigencies of reading and writing call for standard English and there are virtually no voices in the black community calling for newspapers and textbooks, to say nothing of carpenters' manuals, written in Black English.

The existence of standard English is not the result of a political conspiracy "to keep the black man down." But rather standardization is a socio-linguistic fact of life. Societies are socially stratified -- whether the organization is a clan, a tribe or a nation-state. It would be nice to think that there are complex, socially stratified societies where the spectrum of standard language is so broad as to include all the different grammars and usages of persons speaking the many varieties of that language under the label of "standard." Sad to say, human behavior just doesn't operate like that. To date, wherever research has been done -- in Europe, Asia and Africa -- this has not been the case. One variety of the language invariably becomes the standard -- the variety that has grammar books written in it, the one for which an orthography is established, the one that is studied by the populace in school. Language standardization appears to be a universal aspect of language variation in a national context -- particularly one involving literacy. There is standard English, standard Arabic, standard Yoruba and standard Hausa, just to note a few. Standardization is not a political invention of racist whites to exploit the Negro, rob him of his heritage, and denigrate his language.

The second fallacy of the "don't teach standard English"
argument is the implication that in the process of learning
standard English, the black child will necessarily be taught
to devalue his "native tongue" -- non-standard vernacular.
There is no reason to assume that a child cannot learn several
dialects of English, and where it is appropriate to use them,
without weakening his self-confidence, self-identity and
racial pride.

Another problem with such an argument is that it over-
looks the point that in refusing to teach standard English to
these children we cut off even further their possibility of
entering the mainstream of American life.[6]

And finally, not teaching the black inner-city child
standard English not only further hinders his ability to ultimately compete in the mainstream of society in terms of oral
skills, but also makes the child's task of learning to read
considerably more difficult.[7]

It seems clear from the discussion above that it is
necessary to teach standard English to non-standard speakers.
They must know the language of the country if they are to become a part of the mainstream of that society. The need for
teaching standard English to these children, however, does
not rule out the use of non-standard English within the classroom. It does not contradict the call for new, more meaning-
ful curricula for these children, nor does it exonerate past
failures on the part of the school system. It simply re-
affirms the goal of the school system to turn out literate
citizens who can compete in and contribute to the mainstream
culture. In order to do this the school must teach all
children the language of the mainstream.

Who Should Teach Standard English to Black Children?

Once it is determined that it is necessary to teach
black children standard English, the question arises as to
who should do this. Who in the school system is prepared to

deal with this problem? At the present time there is no individual department in the school system that can deal with it.

Some English teachers, despite their previous training
towards conceptualizing standard English as right and "God
given" and all other dialects as wrong and bad, have begun to
take an interest in the issue of training Negro non-standard
speakers. Some speech teachers, despite their previous tradition of looking at deviance from standard language as
pathology, have begun to express concern over helping black
children learn to speak standard English. Some foreign language teachers with their background in comparative linguistics have also become interested in dealing with the problem
of "second language learning" as it applies to black children
learning to speak standard English. It is my feeling that
from this cadre of interested individuals with their varied
backgrounds a specialist can emerge who will be effective in
coping with the language problems of ghetto youngsters. Such
an interested person, however, must be well-trained. High
motivation and a dedicated soul are not substitutes for competence when it comes to teaching children.

One of the first issues to be dealt with concerning the
teacher is the question: Should the teacher who wishes to
teach black children be black?

Many black nationalists have been insisting that the
teachers of black children be black. What these same nationalists have scrupulously avoided discussing is the fact that
many middle class Negroes (from which, of course, the majority
of black teachers continue to be drawn) are as anti-ghetto
black as the white teachers. They share the white teachers'
ignorance and prejudice toward the black child and his language.[8] They are careful to proclaim that they never spoke
dialect.[9] They, too, believe all the current dogma and
mythology concerning the child's homelife and its consequent
effect on his learning. A black teacher may surely be helpful

to these children in terms of the teacher's own experience
as a black person, but that in itself does not provide any
assurance that the child will learn simply because the teacher is the same color as he (surely the failure of the black
school system is a testament in part to that fact). Just as
high motivation and good intent are not enough, black skin
per se does not insure effective teaching of black children --
competence, which is colorless, is a necessary ingredient for
success.

Developing an Urban Language Specialist

1. The need for a specialist. What does the teacher of
black children have to know? How is she to be trained?

First, a teacher who wishes to work with language and
speech programs for black children must receive training concerning language. What is language? What are dialects? How
do social factors influence language and language learning?
What are the functions of a language? What is the relationship of spoken language to written language and reading?
What is linguistic interference?

Second, she needs specific training in learning the
child's vernacular. What is his language like? More specifically she should learn the dialect.[10] In the process of
learning the dialect, I believe that the teacher will develop
a greater respect for what it is she is asking of her children
and what the difficulties are in learning another system,
especially one which in many ways is superficially comparable
to standard English. In addition, in learning the non-standard
dialect, the teacher will understand that one can learn another
dialect of English without "changing" or "improving" the dialect that one already speaks.

Those teachers who already know the dialect will also
need some of this training so that they can reorient their
notion about Negro dialect, and can specify the areas where
interference from the dialect will affect performance in

standard English. Thus they will be able to anticipate problems as well as prepare lessons for teaching standard English.

Teachers will also have to learn something of foreign
language teaching techniques to aid them in preparing materials
for presentation to children, and some of the evaluation procedures of speech therapy (with specific adaptations in reference to dialect speakers) to help them in assessing their effectiveness and the children's progress. Training of these
teachers must also include discussions of the language arts
curriculum so that their new knowledge can be applied to
making changes in materials and presentations that will aid
in teaching reading and writing skills.

Lastly, these inner-city teachers must be familiar with
the ghetto culture in addition to its distinctive language
patterns. In talking about familiarity with ghetto culture
one must be careful not to confuse psychological and sociological data with its emphasis on normative behavior for
ethnological fact. For example, the sociological fact that
there is quite often no "man in the house" does not give us
much information concerning what a ghetto family really is
like.. Perhaps the best example of confusing psychological
data (interpreted on the basis of a false premise-deficit
thesis) for reality is the history of the professional con-
ceptualization of the ghetto child's linguistic competence.[11]
Since most people take the psychological data on face value
they presume that ghetto black children are verbally desti-
tute and are truly amazed when they discover that verbal ability is highly regarded in the ghetto; ability to "sound" is
important and that the man of words is given considerable
status by his compatriots.[12] Black children in elementary
school are busy becoming proficient in the various toasts and
in playing the dozens[13] even if they are all but mute when it
comes to dealing with standard English situations in the
classroom. The teacher must be aware of the different

learning styles of ghetto youth and how they may affect the
way material should be presented.[14]

Obviously the teacher who is to work in the black inner-
city schools, and who is to institute new curricula with
teaching styles suited for black children will have to be
provided with a training program which incorporates the content described above. Such a specialist with this kind of
training is sorely needed.

2. Programs and materials available. Granting that it
is necessary for a specialist to teach standard English to
non-standard speakers, and given the fact that from various
disciplines an individual can be trained to work with these
children what kind of program should be instituted? What
does the trained specialist do? First let us look generally
at what has been done in the past and then discuss what needs
to be done, and what the problems are that must be overcome
in order to do the job well.

Speech and language programs have been devised that
focused on the language abilities of preschoolers, elementary
and secondary students, drop-outs and adult "new careers"
people.

The preschool programs are best represented by the intervention programs known generally as "head start." The programs were developed on a deficit model, and most program
directors believed that they were teaching these children
language (not a second language). These programs were generally of two types:

a. Enrichment - here it was presumed that the language
of the black child was underdeveloped due to lack of stimula-
tion, poor mothering, etc., and the program was designed to
compensate for this. The children learned about neighborhood
workers, the friendly policeman, colors, nursery rhymes, etc.
The best of the middle class nursery school was presented to
these children.

b. Academic - the now famous Bereiter and Engelmann[15]
approach. These intervention programs were not based on
under-development of skills but rather on a presumed absence
of the skills. These programs attempted to teach the children
language arts[16] and mathematic skills through formalized instruction.

Since one of the avowed purposes of these early childhood intervention programs was to "improve language skills"
(tacitly defined in these programs as teaching the child to
speak standard English) one would have to say the programs
were a failure in that there are no data to indicate that
following a preschool intervention program, these children
were more proficient speakers of standard English.[17]

Despite the failure of these preschool programs to improve the black child's command of standard English, due
largely to a lack of knowledge of what language is and how
children learn language, the question still remains as to
whether a child can be taught standard English as a "quasi
foreign language" at the preschool level. With adequately
trained teachers and special materials perhaps the question
of the optimal period for teaching these children standard
English can be discerned. However, the optimal period for
teaching children a second dialect still remains to be determined.

The junior high and high school programs have generally
been zeroed in on as "prime-times" to teach standard English
as a second language to black children. The problem with
many of these programs is that they use the jargon of second
language teaching but actually have as their goal the replacement of what they consider a substandard system (Negro
non-standard English which they give credence to as a legitimate system but to which they assign secondary status) with
standard English.[18]

A prototype of such a program is Ruth Golden's "Improving Patterns of Language Usage." Although Mrs. Golden asserts that Negroes in low socioeconomic classes use non-standard language patterns, she goes on to say that these patterns are "antiquated and awkward in structure." Further, she indicates that Negro non-standard English is inferior since the "level of language (Negro non-standard English) which has served very well for their parents is inadequate for them (Negro students)."[19] Despite the fact that she says the language patterns of Negro students ought not be solely those of the Negro community (implying more than one system) she actually feels that they should be solely standard English speakers as evidence by her disappointment that "...many students who can speak well in class are not sufficiently motivated to continue in an acceptable (to her) informal pattern, but often revert to substandard as soon as they leave the classroom." Her misinterpretation of the students' appropriate use of two language systems (standard English for the classroom and Negro non-standard English for the peer group) as "insufficient motivation for using standard English" clearly indicates that her program is one of eradication of old patterns and replacement with acceptable patterns.

Mrs. Golden's program, as with most of the teaching English as a second language to Negro non-standard English speakers programs, relies on pattern practice as the modus operandi for acquiring standard English. The programs generally do not use contrastive techniques but rather rely simply on repetition of standard English patterns.

Nevertheless, programs have been initiated that genuinely respect the language of the student and that attempt to teach standard English using contrastive techniques.[20] The materials developed at the Center for Applied Linguistics provide one example of such a program.[21] This program not only implicitly recognizes the legitimacy of the students'

system but also uses both standard and non-standard constructions in instruction and drill techniques. With such a
teaching system, the student learns not only what standard
English is but also how and where it differs from non-standard
English.

This technique is extremely important when dealing with
teaching English as a "quasi-foreign language" and serves to
underline one of the main differences between second language
teaching and second dialect teaching. In second language
teaching the language to be learned is distinct enough from
the students' own system so that he knows, for example, he is
speaking French, whether well or poorly, and not English.
In second dialect learning this is not always so and in many
instances the student does not know where non-standard English
leaves off and standard English begins. Therefore he quite
often may not be sure, unless he is specifically instructed,
when he is using standard English and when he is using forms
that appear to be standard English. For example, in Negro
non-standard English he working would mean that he is working
right now, whereas he be working means he is working repeat-
edly over a period of time. In standard English he is working
can be used for cases both of immediacy and of duration. If
the Negro non-standard English speaker is instructed to use
he is working without explicitly discussing the different uses
in standard English and Negro non-standard English, he may use
he is working for immediate situations only (therefore really
not speaking standard English though using standard English
forms) and may hypercorrect he be working to he bees working
to denote a kind of duration.

Unfortunately the Center for Applied Linguistics' materials, although based on a more sophisticated understanding of
language and a quite thorough knowledge of both standard English and Negro non-standard English (like many of the "second
language learning" programs for Negro inner-city children),

have not been evaluated in a teaching context. However, the
Center materials have the distinct advantage of having been
developed in the field situation and used in the classroom,
and thus the course developers were able to get initial im-
pressions concerning the efficiency and effectiveness of their
lessons.

If we presume that materials to teach standard English
as a second dialect can be developed and that specialists can
be trained to teach with them and to generate more material,
the question still remains how shall such a specialist be
incorporated into the school system. It seems that the answer
to such a question depends upon the level at which the new
material is introduced.

Teaching the details of standard English in junior high
and high school might well be treated as a separate course.
Kenneth Johnson has indicated that teaching standard English
as a separate subject as opposed to incorporating it within
the existing language arts curriculum may well be the most
effective approach.[22] Giving the specialist the role of
standard English teacher with emphasis on oral language pro-
ficiency clearly denotes a function in the same way that the
French teacher's role is identifiable. In the same way that
the French teacher must be trained in second language techniques, French language, French culture and history, the
standard English teacher must be trained in second language
techniques, Negro non-standard English and Afro-American
culture and history. The standard English teacher, unlike
the English teacher who wishes to teach the formal aspects
of a language as well as stylistic conventions--i.e. the
business letter, the essay, etc.--to students who already
know the language, understands her job as teaching standard
English to non-standard English speakers. She does not assume they know the language she is teaching.

3. The role of the specialist. What the role of the

specialist in the preschool and elementary school should be
is less clear. If we had a distinct bilingual situation
here, one might suggest that the specialist actually teach
the primary grades in Negro non-standard English while incorporating procedures for teaching standard English into
the curriculum. However, one of the distinctions between a
school which must deal with children who speak a different
language as opposed to a school where a different dialect is
taught involves mutual intelligibility. A class full of non-
English speaking children with a teacher who speaks only
English will no doubt have to resort to gestures and pictures
in order to function at all. This is not true in the case of
Negro non-standard English speaking children and a standard
English speaking teacher. With a little bit of tuning in on
both the teacher and the children's part and with a shared
vocabulary the classroom is able to "function" from the very
beginning although they speak differently. However, con-
tinued failure of many black inner-city schools indicates
that this kind of functioning is not adequate.

The most effective use of the specialist at the primary
level might be as classroom teacher. In this role she could
use her knowledge of Negro non-standard English to teach the
child standard English and to aid the child in his initial
attempts to read.[23] Although she would use standard English
as the medium of instruction (except when she is contrasting
standard English and Negro non-standard English) she would
allow the children to use Negro non-standard English in re-
sponding (except of course when she was teaching standard
English) thereby not confusing knowledge of standard English
with knowledge of the subject matter -- science, math, etc.
to be learned.[24] As the child progressed through the primary
grades and became more proficient in standard English, use of
more standard English could be demanded within the classroom.
Such an approach would allow the child to learn the expected

language response system before he was required to use it.
Of course, a program such as the one discussed above is pro-
mulgated on the assumption that it is both possible and efficient to teach young children standard English using a
"quasi foreign language" approach. This assumption should
be tested.

Conclusion

This paper has attempted to deal with some of the issues
involved in educating black children who do not speak standard English. Questions have been raised concerning whether
these children should learn standard English, who should
teach them, how a specialist should be trained and what such
specialists should do. This author firmly believes that the
success of black children in our public school system is very
much dependent upon the teacher's recognition of the fact
that these children may not speak standard English, and that
if they do not speak standard English, formal instruction in
the language arts cannot continue to be predicated on the
assumption that all the children know standard English. The
dialect of black non-standard speaking children must be incorporated into the curriculum as part of the process of
teaching these children standard English skills. Only then
can such a child learn a second dialect (standard English)
without experiencing shame and humiliation towards his native
dialect.

NOTES

1.   Bernstein, B. Social class, linguistic codes and gram-
     matical elements, Language and Speech, 5, 1962, 221-240.
     Studies have proliferated from Bernstein's writings that
     take his assumptions and hypotheses concerning language
     and categorically turn them into a taxonomy of lower
     class speech. For example, studies that show greater use
     of pronouns in lower class than in middle class speech
     have been erroneously interpreted to indicate greater
     abstraction on the part of middle class speakers. On the
     contrary, there is no research to indicate saying "The

big red fire engine drove through the street," is any
more abstract than saying "It drove through the street."
Speech style is being confused with (and substituted for)
language abstraction. Bereiter perhaps is most glaring
in his "bastardization" of Bernstein when he suggests
that if the child "does not know the word not...he is
deprived of one of the most powerful tools of our language." (Bereiter, C.E., Academic instruction and preschool children, in Corbin, R. and Crosby, M., (eds.)
Language Programs for the Disadvantaged, National Council
of Teachers of English, Champaign, Ill., 1965). Although
the Negro child does not use not - i.e. "this is not a
book," he does use "ain't no" - i.e. "that ain't no book"
which is no less powerfully logical!

2. Erikson, Fredrick, "F'get You Honky!": A new look at
black dialect in school, Elementary English, 46, No. 4,
1969, 495-499.

3. Taken from Labov, W., The logic of non-standard, The
Florida FL Reporter, Spring, 1969, 60-74, 169. Also
printed in Alatis, J. (ed.), Monograph Series on Languages and Linguistics (20th Annual Round Table Meeting),
Georgetown University Press, Washington, D.C., 1969,
1-45. For a discussion of the problems of employing a
deficit model see Baratz and Baratz, Early childhood
intervention: The social science basis of institutional
racism, Harvard Educational Review, Winter, 1970.

4. Wayne O'Neil (Paul Roberts' rules of order: The misuse of
linguistics in the classroom, The Urban Review, 2, No. 7,
1968, pp. 12, 17) insists that "instead of 'enriching'
the lives of urban children by plugging them into a
'second' dialect...we should be working to eradicate the
language prejudice, the language mythology, that people
grew into holding and believing." Although I agree with
Mr. O'Neil that something should be done concerning misconceptions about language in the educational establish-
ment, I do not feel that this should be done instead of
second dialect teaching but rather in addition to the
second dialect training for Negro ghetto children.
Learning the mainstream tongue is as important for the
black child as is eradicating the misconceptions in both
the white and black community concerning this original
dialect.

5. The pejorative ratings of Negro non-standard English by
most blacks is a factor which must be taken into account
here. Negro self hate is perhaps a more potent force
today than white oppression, in the denial of the worth
of Negro dialect. For more information on attitudes
toward Negro non-standard speech see Shuy, Roger W.,

Baratz, Joan C., and Wolfram, Walter A., Sociolinguistic
factors in speech identification - Final report,
MH15048-01, NIMH, 1969.

6. I do not wish to suggest that the use of standard English
by black children will insure their success in middle
class white America or that it will erase prejudice
against Negroes, nevertheless, since standard English is
the language of the mainstream it seems clear that knowledge of the mainstream system increases the likelihood
of success in the mainstream culture.

7. Study after study has demonstrated that children with a
different language system from that of the national language have a great deal of difficulty learning to read
when taught to read in the national tongue (UNESCO Conference on World Literacy, 1953). The Negro non-standard
speaker trying to learn to read with a standard English
text is in much the same position as children learning
to read a language other than the one they speak. For
further discussion of this issue see, Baratz, J. and
Shuy, R. Teaching Black Children to Read, Center for
Applied Linguistics, Washington, D.C., 1969.

8. It was a Negro, Charles Hurst, Jr., who coined the now
disreputable term "dialectolalia" which he defined as an
abnormal speech pattern characterized by "oral aberra-
tions such as phonemic and sub-phonemic replacements,
segmental phonemes, phonemic distortions, defective syntax, misarticulations, limited and poor vocabulary, and
faulty phonology. These variables exist commonly in
unsystematic multifarious combinations." (Hurst, Charles,
Psychological Correlates in Dialectolalia, Cooperative
Research Project #2610, Communication Sciences and Research Center, Howard University, 1965.

9. At a recent talk on Negro non-standard, I noticed two
Negro teachers who stood in the doorway and assured all
departing whites that "they always spoke this way" (in
standard English).

10. Learning a foreign language is not the same as learning
a second dialect. The literature in verbal learning has
indicated again and again that it is harder to learn
material that is quite familiar than it is to learn two
sets of distinct material.

11. See Baratz, J., The language of the economically dis-
advantaged· child: A perspective, ASHA, 1968 and Language
and cognitive assessment of negro children: Assumptions
and research needs, ASHA, 1969.

12. See for example, Ulf Hannerz' Walking my walk and talk-
    ing my talk, in Hannerz, U., Soulside: Inquiries into
    Ghetto Culture and Community, Columbia University Press,
    New York, 1969.

13. Playing the dozens, joining, sounding, rapping are terms
    for distinct verbal styles in the ghetto. For more in-
    formation see Abrahams, R., Deep Down in the Jungle,
    Hatboro, Pa. Folklore Associates, 1964; Kochman, T.,
    "Rapping" in the Black Ghetto, Transaction, 1969,
    pp. 26-34; Labov, W. et al., A study of the non-standard
    English of negro and Puerto Rican speakers in New York
    City, Cooperative Research Project No. 3288, Volume II,
    The Use of Language in the Speech Community, Columbia
    University, 1968.

14. Some excellent beginning work on differences in cognitive
    styles in different ethnic groups can be found in
    Lesser, G. and Stodolsky, S., Learning patterns in the
    disadvantaged, Harvard Educational Review, 37, No. 4,
    1967.

15. Bereiter, C. and Engelmann, S., Teaching Disadvantaged
    Children in the Preschool, Prentice-Hall, Englewood
    Cliffs, N.J., 1967.

16. Language arts involved formal instruction in the authors'
    concept of oral standard English and in beginning reading.

17. Almost all of the data presented to date (see for example,
    Klaus and Gray, The early training project for disad-
    vantaged children: A report after five years, Monograph
    of the Society for Research in Child Development, 33,
    1968) involve shifts (and transitory at that since they
    do not appear to be sustained once the child enters
    school) in IQ scores.

18. See for example Ruth Golden's Improving Patterns of
    Language Usage, Wayne State University Press, Detroit,
    1960 or Virginia French Allen, Learning a second dia-
    lect is not learning another language, Monograph Series
    on Languages and Linguistics, 20th Annual Roundtable
    Meeting, Georgetown University Press, Washington, D.C.,
    1969, 189-202, where despite using second language
    learning analogy Mrs. Allen concludes with an anecdote
    concerning the fact that the child is "worth revising".

19. Golden, R., Improving Patterns of Language Usage, Wayne
    State University Press, Detroit, 1960.

20. See for example Gladney, M. and Leaverton, L., A model
    for teaching standard English to nonstandard English

speakers, <u>AERA</u> paper, 1968, for contrastive approach with young children or Johnson, K., An evaluation of second language techniques for teaching standard English to negro students, <u>NCTE</u> paper, 1968, for use with older students.

21. The materials, <u>English Now</u>, developed by Irwin Feigenbaum are currently being published by New Century.

22. Johnson, K. An evaluation of second language techniques for teaching standard English to negro students, <u>NCTE</u> paper, 1968.

23. The Education Study Center is currently involved in a reading project in the District of Columbia using dialect texts as initial readers.

24. I remember being in a third grade class that was discussing the Revolutionary War. The teacher asked "Who crossed the Delaware River with troops? A young Negro boy responded "Dat George Washington" to which the teacher replied "No, that was George Washington." With such a correction the class, I am sure, was confused as to the right answer and the boy learned not to volunteer information again!

SOME LINGUISTIC FEATURES OF NEGRO DIALECT

by Ralph W. Fasold and Walt Wolfram

There are essentially three sources of information on the
features of Negro dialect.[1] First, there are detailed technical linguistic analyses which are difficult for non-
specialists to read. Another source of information is in
the form of lists which usually sacrifice adequacy in favor
of simplicity. A third source of information is articles
about the history of Negro dialect in which certain features
are emphasized, but in which no comprehensive analysis is
attempted. Our purpose here is to present the information
currently available on the linguistic features of Negro dialect in non-technical language, but in sufficient detail to
be useful, if not to teachers themselves, at least to those
who would like to write teaching materials but do not feel
secure in their knowledge of the features involved. The
details of the analysis being presented are based on careful
research and while no extensive references to this research
are made in the course of the presentation, all the source
material can be found in the bibliography.

Before discussing the features themselves, it is necessary to clarify several facts about Negro dialect. First,
it should be understood that not all Negroes speak Negro dialect. There are many Negroes whose speech is indistinguishable from others of the same region and social class, and
there are many whose speech can be identified as Negro only
by a few slight differences in pronunciation and vocal quality.
Second, Negro dialect shares many features with other kinds of

English. Its distinctiveness, however, lies in the fact that
it has a number of pronunciation and grammatical features
which are not shared by other dialects. It is important to
realize that Negro dialect is a fully formed linguistic system in its own right, with its own grammar and pronunciation
rules; it cannot simply be dismissed as an unworthy approxi-
mation of standard English. In fact, there are some grammatical distinctions which can be made more easily in Negro
dialect than in standard English. Negro dialect, then, as
the term is used here, is a cohesive linguistic system which
is substantially different from standard American English
dialects. It is spoken by some, though not all Negroes, particularly those of the lower socioeconomic classes. Furthermore, as will be brought out in the discussion, almost all
the features associated with Negro dialect alternate with
standard English forms in actual speech. To avoid forming
a distorted picture of how speech is actually used in the
lower socioeconomic black community, this variation or alternation should be kept in mind when reading the descriptions
which follow.

     There are two possible reasons for the distinctiveness
of Negro dialect, one being the fact that the linguistic
history of the dialect is partly independent from the history
of the rest of American English. It has been postulated
that several of the features of the dialect are traceable,
not to British dialects, but to African languages via the
Caribbean Creole languages. Even if this is not the case,
the persistent segregation patterns of our society are sufficient cause for Negro dialect to develop its own character.
Dialects develop when speakers of a common language are separated from each other, either by geographical or social distance. The social distance between white and black Americans
must be cited as a contributing factor to the maintenance and
development of distinct dialect features.

PRONUNCIATION

It is important to keep separate the two kinds of differences between standard English and Negro dialect. Some of these features, like the pronunciation of then as den, are the result of differences in the pronunciation systems of two kinds of American English. Other differences, like the use of "double" or multiple negatives, are grammatical in nature. Sometimes it is not obvious which kind of feature is involved. For example, we will see that the rule which causes speakers of Negro dialect to say He go where standard English speakers say He goes is a grammatical rule. On the other hand, the rule by which speakers of Negro dialect say He walk where standard dialect speakers say He walked is a pronunciation rule. Some of the reasons for this conclusion and for the importance of the distinction between the two types of rules will be given in the description to follow.

Word-final Consonant Clusters

1. General. Standard English words ending in a consonant cluster or blend often have the final member of the cluster absent in Negro dialect.[2] As we shall see, the reduction of some clusters which are formed by the addition of the -s suffix can be attributed to a grammatical difference between standard English and Negro dialect (see pp. 63, 76-78). Other types of cluster "reductions", however, do not result from grammatical differences, but are the product of pronunciation differences in final consonant clusters. In Negro dialect, words such as test, desk, hand, and build are pronounced as tes', des', han', and buil' respectively. Because of this, we find that pairs of words such as build and bill, coal and cold, and west and Wes have identical pronunciations in Negro dialect.

It is important to distinguish two basic types of clusters which are affected by this sort of reduction. First of all, clusters in which both members of the cluster belong to

the same "base word" can be reduced, as in tes', des', han',
and buil'. But reduction also affects final t or d which
results when the suffix -ed is added to the "base word."[3]
In all varieties of English, the -ed suffix has several different phonetic forms, depending on how the base word ends.
If it ends in d or t, the -ed suffix is pronounced something
like id (e.g. wantid, countid); otherwise it is pronounced
as t or d. When the word ends in a voiced sound, it is pronounced as d, so that words with -ed like rubbed or rained
are actually pronounced as rubd and raind respectively. Consonants like b, n, and g are pronounced with vocal chords
vibrating, that is, they are voiced. If the base word ends
in a voiceless consonant, the cluster ends in t, so that
messed and looked are actually pronounced as mest and lookt,
respectively. Consonants such as s, k, and f are pronounced
without the vibration of the vocal chords, that is, they are
voiceless. In Negro dialect, when the addition of the -ed
suffix results in either a voiced or voicless cluster, the
cluster may be reduced by removing the final member of the
cluster. This affects -ed when it functions as a past tense
marker (e.g. Yesterday he move' away), a participle (e.g.
The boy was mess' up) or an adjective (e.g. He had a scratch'
arm), although its association with the past tense is the
most frequent. The list of clusters affected by this process
and the examples of the two types of consonant cluster reduction are given in the following table: Type I represents
clusters which do not involve -ed and Type II represents
clusters which result from the addition of the -ed suffix.

    Note that in the table, such clusters as [mp] (e.g.
jump, ramp), [nt] (e.g. count, rent), [lt] (e.g. colt, belt),
[ŋk] (e.g. crank, rank), and [lp] (e.g. gulp, help) are not
included. The reason is that the reduction rule operates
only when both members of the cluster are either voiced or
voiceless. Words like mind, cold, or rained (pronounced

Table 1

Consonant Clusters in which the Final Member
of the Cluster may be Absent

Phonetic
Cluster   Examples*

	Type I	Type II
[st]	test, post, list	missed, messed, dressed
[sp]	wasp, clasp, grasp	
[sk]	desk, risk, mask	
[št]		finished, latched, cashed
[zd]		raised, composed, amazed
[žd]		judged, charged, forged
[ft]	left, craft, cleft	laughed, stuffed, roughed
[vd]		loved, lived, moved
[nd]	mind, find, mound	rained, fanned, canned
[md]		named, foamed, rammed
[ld]	cold, wild, old	called, smelled, killed
[pt]	apt, adept, inept	mapped, stopped, clapped
[kt]	act, contact, expect	looked, cooked, cracked

*Where there are no examples under Type I or II, the cluster
does not occur under that category.

---

raind) end in two voiced sounds, n and d. On the other hand,
words like jump, count, belt, crank, and help end in one
voiced and one voiceless sound; m, n, l and the [ŋ] sound are
voiced, while t, k and p are voiceless. Since final consonant clusters can be reduced only when both consonants are
voiced or when both consonants are voiceless, these words ending in one of each kind of consonant never have reduced
clusters.

     In some ways, the absence of the final member of the
consonant cluster in Negro dialect is like a process which
can also be observed in standard English; in other ways,
however, it is quite different. In standard English, the

final member of the cluster may be absent if the following
word begins with a consonant, so that bes' kind, col' cuts,
and wes' side are common and acceptable in spoken standard
English.[4] In standard English, however, this reduction can
take place only when the following word begins with a consonant. While col' cuts, does not violate the pronunciation
rules of standard English, col' egg does. In Negro dialect,
this reduction not only takes place when the following word
begins with a consonant, but it may also take place when it
is followed by a vowel or a pause of some type. Thus wes'
en', bes' apple, or col' egg are all acceptable according to
Negro dialect rules of pronunciation. Items such as Yesterday
he was mess' up occur because of this pronunciation rule and
not because past tense is absent in Negro dialect. In standard English it is not at all unusual to hear a sentence such
as Yesterday I burn' my hand, since the potential cluster in
burned is followed by a word beginning with a consonant. But
a sentence such as It was burn' up, acceptable in Negro dialect, would not be acceptable in standard English since the
potential cluster is followed by a word beginning with a
vowel.

2. Plural formation. Related to the reduction of final
consonant clusters in Negro dialect is a particular pattern
of pluralization involving the -s and -es plural forms. In
all varieties of English, there are several different phonetic
forms for the plural suffix. If the word ends in an s-like
sound (i.e. a sibilant such as s, sh, z, zh), the plural suffix is formed by adding -es; phonetically, this is pronounced
something like -iz. Thus bus, bush, and buzz are pluralized
as buses, bushes, and buzzes respectively. If the word does
not end in an s-like sound, then -s is added; phonetically
this is z after voiced sounds and s after voiceless sounds.
Thus, the plural of pot, coat, bud, and pan is pots, coats,
buds (phonetically budz) and pans (phonetically panz)

respectively. In Negro dialect, words ending in s plus p, t or k add the -es plural instead of the -s plural.[5] Thus, words like desk, ghost, wasp, and test are pluralized as desses, ghoses, wasses, and tesses. Because the p, t, and k are so often removed by the rule discussed above, these plurals are formed as if desk, test, and wasp ended in s, instead of sk, st, or sp. It is essential to understand that this is a regular pluralization pattern due to the status of final consonant clusters in Negro dialect.

Attempting to learn standard English pluralization patterns, speakers will sometimes pluralize words like desk and test as deskes and testes respectively. These forms result from the failure to eliminate Negro dialect pluralization after realizing that words like test and desk are to be pronounced with a cluster. Technically, this is known as "hypercorrection".

3. The status of word-final clusters. Because consonant clusters occur so infrequently at the end of words in Negro dialect, one might ask whether these word-final clusters can be considered an integral part of the Negro dialect system. That is, are speakers of Negro dialect at all familiar with what words may and what words may not end in clusters? This question is crucial for teaching, since clusters must be taught as completely new items if Negro dialect speakers are completely unfamiliar with them. On the other hand, if clusters are a part of the dialect and simply different from standard English because they can undergo reduction in certain contexts where reduction is not possible in standard English (e.g. when the following word begins with a vowel), the teaching problem is of a different nature. What must be taught in the latter case, is the contexts in which cluster reduction is not possible in standard English but is possible in Negro dialect, while the lists of standard English words ending in clusters must be taught as completely new items if clusters are not an integral part of the dialect.

This question can be answered most clearly by observing
what happens when suffixes beginning with a vowel are added
to a base word ending in a cluster in standard English. This
includes -ing as in testing or scolding, -er as in tester or
scolder and -est as in coldest or oldest. If a consonant
cluster is present in such constructions (e.g. testing,
tester), we may assume that the speaker is fully acquainted
with the cluster, but that it can be reduced in places where
it is not possible in standard English. For the vast majority of Negro dialect speakers in the North, this is exactly
how the rule concerning consonant clusters operates. These
speakers may reduce the cluster in the context of tes'
program or tes' idea, but retain the cluster in tester.
There is, however, also a group of Negro dialect speakers,
most typically Southern children, who not only show the absence of the final member of the cluster in tes' program or
tes' idea, but in teser as well. For these speakers, the
teaching of standard English must start with the list of
standard English words which end in consonant clusters.

We may summarize our observations about the word-final
consonant clusters in the following table, which represents
how standard English and the two varieties of Negro dialect
function with respect to final consonant clusters. The three
contexts mentioned above are: (1) the following word begins
with a consonant, (2) the following word does not begin with
a consonant, and (3) a suffix beginning with a vowel follows.

Table 2

Consonant Cluster Reduction

	(1) ___#C	(2) ___#	(3) ___-V
Standard English	tes' program	test idea	testing
Negro dialect 1	tes' program	tes' idea	testing
Negro dialect 2	tes' program	tes' idea	tes'ing

On the basis of this table, we can draw some general con-
clusions about the social significance of consonant cluster
reduction. We see, for example, that Negro dialect is very
much like standard English when the following word begins with
a consonant; a reduction of the cluster therefore has little
social significance in this context. When not followed by a
consonant, however, it is socially stigmatized. Absence of
the cluster is most stigmatized when a suffix beginning with
a vowel is added.

The th-Sounds

1. General. In standard English, the letters th actually represent two different types of sound. First, they
represent the voiced sound in words such as the, they, and
that (i.e. a voiced interdental fricative). Second, they
represent the voiceless sound as in words like thought, thin,
and think (a voiceless interdental fricative). In Negro dialect, the regular pronunciation rules for the sounds represented by th are quite different. The particular sounds which
th represents are mainly dependent on the context in which th
occurs. That is, the sounds for th are dependent on where th
might occur in a word and/or what sounds occur next to it.

2. Word-initial. At the beginning of a word, the th in
the is frequently pronounced as a d in Negro dialect, so that
words such as the, they, and that are pronounced as de, dey,
and dat respectively. It has been pointed out that a limited
amount of d for th is also characteristic of standard English
in the most casual or informal speech style. In Negro dialect, however, it is much more frequent so that the pronunciation de for the is the regular pronunciation. It is important to note here that the pronunciation of d for th in
Negro dialect is not simply an error in pronunciation, but
the result of a regular and patterned rule.

In the case of th in words such as thought, think or
thin (the voiceless interdental fricative), th is sometimes

pronounced as t, so that thought, think or thin are pronounced
as tought, tink and tin respectively. However, most Negro
dialect speakers who pronounce thought as tought will also
sometimes pronounce it as thought. That is, both the th and
t pronunciations for thought are appropriate for Negro dialect. If th is followed by r as in throat or three still
another pronunciation is possible. These words may be pronounced with an f, so that three and throat can be pronounced
as free and froat respectively. This means that items such
as three and free may be pronounced the same in Negro dialect.

3. Within a word. In the middle of the word, there are
several different pronunciations for th in Negro dialect.
For the voiceless sound as in nothing, author, or ether, most
frequently it is pronounced as f. Thus, nothing, author, and
ether are pronounced as nuf'n, ahfuh, and eefuh respectively.
For the voiced sound, as in brother, rather or bathing, th is
pronounced as v in some varieties of Negro dialect, so that
these words are pronounced as bruvah, ravah, and bavin',
respectively.

In addition to f and v for th in the middle of a word,
several other pronunciations may occur. When th is followed
by a nasal sound such as m or n, th may be pronounced as t.
Thus 'ritmetic for arithmetic, nut'n for nothing or montly for
monthly, are patterns frequently used in Negro dialect. There
are also several items in which no consonant at all is found.
For example, mother may be pronounced as muh (with a lengthened
vowel) and brother may be pronounced as bruh. This pattern,
however, is relatively infrequent and only takes place when
the vowel sounds preceding and following th are similar.

4. Word-final. At the end of a word, f is the pre-
dominant pronunciation of th in words such as Ruth, tooth,
and south, which are pronounced as Ruf, toof, and souf,
respectively. Whereas most speakers fluctuate between the
pronunciation of f and th in the middle of the word, some

speakers exclusively use f and v at the ends of these words.
In addition to f and v at the ends of these words, several
other sounds may be represented by th, dependent upon the
sounds which precede it.[6]   When the preceding sound is the
nasal sound n, t may occur so that tenth and month are pronounced as tent' and mont', respectively. The stop t or d
may also be used with the preposition with, so that it is
pronounced as wit or wid. Next to the nasal n, it is also
possible to have no consonant at all present. This means
that month and tenth may be pronounced as mon' and ten'.

r and l

1. After vowels. The pronunciation rule for r and l in
Negro dialect operates in a way quite similar to white speech
in certain parts of the South. At the beginning of a word,
r and l are always pronounced, as in run, lip, rub, or lamp.
In other positions, however, r and l are sometimes reduced to
a vowel-like quality pronounced something like uh. The most
important context to recognize in discussing the so-called
"loss" of r and l is when they follow a vowel (technically
called "post-vocalic"). In such items as steal, sister,
nickel, or bear, only a "phonetic vestige" of r or l is pronounced, so that we hear steauh, sistuh, nickuh, and beauh
respectively. Preceding a consonant in a word (e.g. wart,
tart) some speakers do not have any phonetic vestige of r or
l; this means that help and hep and taught and torte may be
pronounced identically by these speakers. In some areas of
the South, Negro dialect may also reveal no vestige of r following the vowels o or u. For these speakers, door and doe,
four and foe, and sure and show may be pronounced alike.
Although it has been suggested that l may also be completely
absent at the end of a word following o or u, there seems to
be some small phonetic vestige so that toll and toe or mole
and mow do not sound exactly alike in Negro dialect.

In some "r-less" American English dialects the word which
follows r or l is important in determining whether or not r
and l loss may take place. For example, in the r-less dialect
of New England, r is consistently absent when the following
word begins with a consonant, as in brothuh Mike or fouh
people; when followed by a word that begins with a vowel, the
r is consistently present, as in brother Ed or four apples.
In Negro dialect, however, it may be absent in both types of
contexts, although it is more frequently absent when followed
by a word beginning with a consonant (e.g. fouh people) than
when followed by one beginning with a vowel (e.g. fouh apples).

   2. Between vowels. Not only may r or l be absent when
followed by another word beginning with a vowel, but r absence
is occasionally observed between two vowels within a word.
Thus, it is possible to get Ca'ol, sto'y or ma'y for Carol,
story and marry respectively.

   3. Effect on vocabulary and grammar. The consistent
absence of r at the end of a word has led to several "mergers"
of vocabulary items. That is, because of the similarity of
two words after a particular pronunciation rule has taken
place, one word has assumed the function of what was originally
two words. For example, when the phonetic vestige which re-
places the r is removed, there is only a small difference which
separates they from their or you from your. The forms they
and you can be used as possessive as in It is they book or
It is you book in Negro dialect as a result of this merging
process (cf. Undifferentiated pronouns, p. 77).

   Like r, the loss of l may have important implications for
grammatical functions. The most crucial of these deals with
the loss of l on a contracted form of the future modal will.
We may get a sentence such as Tomorrow I bring the thing for
Tomorrow I'll bring the thing, where will becomes 'll and then
is lost completely. This pronunciation process accounts for
use of be in Negro dialect as an indicator of future time, as

in He be here in a few minutes. The pronunciation rule for
the loss of the contracted form of l takes place most frequently when the following word begins with b, m or w (i.e.
labial sounds).

4. After initial consonants. Before leaving our description of the rules for r and l in Negro dialect, we must note
that in certain words, r may be absent when it follows a consonant. Two main types of contexts can be cited to account
for this phonemenon. First, r may be absent when the following vowel is either o or u, so that we get th'ow for throw,
and th'ough for through. Second, r may be absent in unstressed
syllables, so that protéct and proféssor are pronounced as
p'otéct and p'oféssuh, respectively.

5. Social stigma. On the whole, r and l absence has not
been as socially stigmatized as many other grammatical and
pronunciation rules of Negro dialect. This is probably due
to the fact that certain types of r absence are generally
recognized as legitimate regional characterisitcs of some dialects of standard English. Because of the relatively slight
stigmatization, the rule for r and l absence is often found
in the speech of middle class Negroes living in regions characterized by the presence of r and l.

Final b, d, and g

1. Devoicing. At the end of a syllable, the voiced
stops b, d, and g (and, to a lesser extent, all voiced consonants except nasals r, l, w and y) are often pronounced as
the corresponding voiceless stops, p, t, and k, respectively.
This means that words such as pig, bud, and cab end in k, t,
and p, respectively. Before concluding that pig and pick,
bud and butt, and cab and cap sound identical in Negro dialect, it is essential to note that they are still distinguished
by the length of the vowel. English vowels are held slightly
longer when the following sound is voiced (i.e. the vowel in
bud is held slightly longer than the vowel in butt). In the

case of Negro dialect, the vowel is lengthened before sounds
such as d in bud, even though the d is actually pronounced t.
As a result, bud does not sound the same as butt because the
u is "stretched out" a little in bud but not in butt.

In some varieties of standard English, "devoicing" can
take place in an unstressed syllable, so that we can get salat
for salad, hundret for hundred, or acit for acid. Negro dialect not only has the rule for devoicing in unstressed syllables, but stressed syllables as well, so that we hear mut
for mud, goot for good and loat for load.

The -ed suffix, when attached to verb bases ending in a
vowel, is represented by d in all varieties of English. The
devoicing rule applies to this d as well as the d of mud, good,
and load. For this reason, played is sometimes pronounced
playt in Negro dialect.

2. Deletion of d. In addition to the devoicing rule,
there are some speakers who may have the complete absence of
the stop d, although this is not nearly as frequent as devoicing. This results in pronunciations such as goo' man and
ba' soldier. The rule for the absence of d occurs more frequently when d is followed by a consonant than when followed
by a vowel (e.g. goo' soldier is more frequent than goo' egg);
d absence is most common before s or z. For this reason, the
addition of an -s suffix often results in pronunciations such
as kiz for kids, and boahz for boards.

d-absence is also possible when d represents the -ed suffix with verbal bases ending in vowels. It is possible to
observe sentences like Yesterday he play it and He had play it
the day before. However, since this rule is much less frequently applied than the rule eliminating the second member of
a consonant cluster, there are many more cases of sentences
like Yesterday he miss it than Yesterday he play it.

Nasalization

There are several different aspects of the nasals m, n,

and ng (phonetically [ŋ]) which must be discussed with reference to Negro dialect. Some of these are quite characteristic
of all nonstandard English dialects, others are characteristic
of southern standard as well as nonstandard dialects, and still
others are unique to Negro dialect.

1. The -ing suffix. The use of the -in suffix for -ing
(e.g. singin', buyin', swimin') is a feature which is characteristic of all socially stigmatized varieties of English. Because of the spelling of [ŋ] as ng this is sometimes referred
to as a "dropping of the g". Although in in such words as
singin', comin' and doin' occurs in all socially stigmatized
varieties of American English, its frequency is somewhat
greater in Negro dialect than in other nonstandard dialects.
In fact, there may be some speakers who do not use the -ing
form at all. This form is one of the most stereotyped phonological features of nonstandard speech in the American language.

2. Nasalized vowels. Another feature which is found in
Negro dialect is the use of a nasalized vowel instead of the
nasal consonant. Generally, this only takes place at the end
of a syllable. In words like man, bun, or bum the final consonant is sometimes not pronounced, but a nasalization of the
preceding vowel is found similar to the type of nasalization
of vowels that is found in a language such as French. This
means that words such as rum, run, and rung might all sound
alike in Negro dialect (that is, they may all be produced as
[rə̃] phonetically where [~] stands for nasalization). As many
other features in Negro dialect, this feature does not occur
categorically. This is, there is always fluctuation between
the use of the nasalized vowel and the nasal consonant.

3. The influence of nasals on i and e. Finally, we
should mention the influence that nasal consonants have on
the vowels i and e. Before a nasal consonant, i and e do not
contrast, making words such as pin and pen or tin and ten

sound identical. This pronunciation rule of Negro dialect is
quite like some standard varieties of Southern speech, and
only has social significance in a Northern context.

Vowel Glides

In some parts of the South, the vowel glides represented
as ay (e.g. side, time) and oy (e.g. boy, toy) are generally
pronounced without the glide. Thus, side and time may be pronounced as sahd and tahm and boy and toy as boah and toah.
This feature of some Southern standard as well as nonstandard
dialects has been adopted as an integral part of Negro dialect. The absence of the glide is much more frequent when it
is followed by a voiced sound or a pause than it is when followed by a voiceless sound. This means that the absence of a
glide is much more likely in words such as side, time, or toy
than it is in kite, bright, or fight. Many speakers never
have a glide when followed by voicing but always have one when
followed by a voiceless sound (e.g. they always have tahm for
time but never have kaht for kite). Because the rule for
vowel glides is found among middle class speakers in the South,
its social significance is limited to Northern areas, where it
ia associated with class and race. Even in Northern areas,
however, its stigmatization is minimal.

Indefinite Articles a and an

In standard English, when the following word begins with
a vowel, the indefinite article an is used as in an apple or
an egg; when it is followed by a word beginning with a consonant, a occurs as in a boy or a dog. In Negro dialect, as
in some varieties of white Southern speech, the article a is
used regardless of how the following word begins. With a
selected group of words (of more than one syllable) which may
begin with a vowel similar to a (phonetically [ə]), the article may also be completely absent (or, at least, "merge" with
the vowel); this results in sentences such as He had eraser
or He had erector set. Less frequently, and mostly among

younger children, this article may be absent in other types
of constructions (e.g. I have pencil), but this type of absence seems to be a grammatical rather than a pronunciation
feature.

Stress

Stress or accent in Negro dialect operates quite like the
stress patterns of standard English with several exceptions.
One exception can be found when standard English words of more
than one syllable have their stress on the second syllable
rather than the first. In Negro dialect, some of these words
may be stressed on the first rather than the second syllable.
This only affects a small subset of words such as políce,
hotél, or Julý, which in Negro dialect are pronounced as
pólice, hótel and Júly.

Another difference which can be traced to stress is
the absence of the first syllable of a word when the first
syllable is unstressed. For example, we find 'rithmetic,
'member, 'cept or 'bout, respectively. Because this pattern
results in the absence of certain types of prefixes, some
speakers may occasionally "overuse" the prefix re-. This
overuse of re- may result in formations such as revorce or
remorial for divorce and memorial, according to William A.
Stewart.

Other Pronunciation Features

In addition to the systematic patterns which have been
mentioned above, there are several features which are quite
restricted. One such feature is the pronunciation of ask as
ax, so that it sounds like axe. This feature, which is quite
prominent in some speakers of Negro dialect, can be related
to an Old English pronunciation which has been preserved in
Negro dialect as well as white Appalachian speech.

Another rule which is quite limited is the absence of s
in a word which ends in x (phonetically [ks]). This pattern
results in the pronunciation of box as bok and six as sik

(homophonous with s<u>i</u>ck). For the most part, this feature is
limited to a few items ending in <u>x</u> and is more frequently
found in Southern speakers of Negro dialect than it is in
Northern speakers.

Finally, we may mention rules for the <u>str</u> clusters in
such words as <u>string</u> and <u>street</u>, which may be pronounced as
<u>skring</u> and <u>skreet</u>, respectively. At the end of a word, <u>st</u>
may also be changed to <u>sk</u>, so that <u>wrist</u> and <u>twist</u> are occasionally pronounced as <u>wrisk</u> and <u>twisk</u> when speakers are trying
to approximate a standard English norm.

There are, of course, other restricted types of differences between the pronunciation rules of Negro dialect and
standard English which might be mentioned. Other examples,
however, are either so limited in terms of the numbers of
items affected or so unobtrusive in terms of their social
significance, that it is sufficient for the teacher to have
a firm understanding of the pronunciation features which we
have described above. Indeed, the teacher who fully understands and respects the pronunciation rules of Negro dialect
discussed here will have taken a necessary step in the effective teaching of standard English.

GRAMMAR

Other features of Negro dialect are due to the fact that
some of the rules of Negro dialect grammar are different from
grammatical rules in standard English. These rules deal with
the verb system, with negation, with noun suffixes, with
question formation, and with pronouns. Some of the features
in the following section, however, are technically pronunciation features, but are described as grammatical features because they are usually perceived as such.

VERBS

Many of the most significant features of Negro dialect
are to be found in its verb system. The differences in the
verb structure of Negro dialect as compared to standard

American English are mainly found in the tense systems of the
two dialects and in their treatment of the verb to be.

Past Forms

   1. The -ed suffix. As we have seen already, the -ed
suffix which marks past tense and past participial forms, as
well as derived adjectives, is sometimes not pronounced in
Negro dialect because of pronunciation rules (pp. 44 and 54).
When -ed is added to a verb base ending in a consonant, as in
missed, it can be removed by application of the consonant
cluster reduction rule. When -ed is added to a verbal base
which ends in a vowel, it can be removed by the rule for
deletion of syllable-final d. As we have already pointed out,
the d-deletion rule applies much less often than the consonant
cluster reduction rule, so that -ed is much more frequently
absent from bases ending in a consonant which is not t or d
than from bases ending in a vowel.

   When -ed is added to a base ending in t or d, it is pronounced something like id[7], as we have mentioned before. In
this form, it is rarely absent in Negro dialect. However,
this id form can be reduced to d alone in Negro dialect and
also in standard English by some fairly complex, but very
regular rules. In casual speech, the words want and start
are the most frequently occurring verbs which are eligible
for these rules. If they apply, the i-sound of id can be
eliminated. The verb then ends in dd or td which is simpli-
fied to d. These operations result in sentences like He stard
crying (from He started crying) and He wanda go (from He wanted
to go). Such sentences are common in all varieties of American
English and are not considered nonstandard. In the case of
stard, Negro dialect (but not standard English) has a rule for
the elimination of the remaining d, especially when the verb
occurs before a gerund, as in He sta crying (the r of start
is absent for reasons we have already discussed). The verb
started is virtually the only verb to undergo this process.[8]

These rules are pronunciation rules. This means that the
missing -ed suffix does not reflect a grammatical difference
between Negro dialect and standard English. The suffix is a
part of the grammar of both kinds of English. Any attempt to
teach the -ed suffix as a grammatical entity, then, will be
superfluous.

Another important implication is that children who speak
Negro dialect should not be required to learn the careful pronunciation of -ed where speakers of standard English usually
do not pronounce it. When -ed is phonetically t or d and is
the second member of a consonant cluster, and when the next
word begins with a consonant, as in Yesterday I burned my hand,
Negro dialect speakers should be allowed to pronounce burned
as burn', the way standard English speakers do.

2. Irregular verbs. Verbs which form their past tenses
in an irregular way distinguish present and past forms in the
overwhelming majority of cases in Negro dialect. The occurrence of sentences like Yesterday he give it to me are rare.
However, some verbs which have irregular past forms in standard English have the same form for past and present tenses in
Negro dialect. There are also such verbs in standard English
(They hit him yesterday; They hit him every day). A few verbs,
notably say, behave like hit for some speakers of Negro dialect, giving, for example, He say it every day; He say it
yesterday. In the case of say, the situation is complicated
by the fact that some speakers who actually use said will be
heard by speakers of standard English as having said say because the d of said has been removed by the word-final d-
elimination rule.

Perfective Constructions

1. General. The perfective constructions in Negro dialect discussed below are first illustrated in Table 3.

Table 3

The Perfective Constructions in Negro Dialect
and Standard English

	Negro Dialect	Standard English
Present Perfect	I have walked I('ve) walked	I have walked I've walked
Past Perfect	I had walked	I had walked I'd walked
Completive	I done walked	
Remote Time	I been walked	

    2. <u>Omission of forms of have</u>. In standard American
English, the present tense forms of auxiliary <u>have</u> can be
contracted to <u>'ve</u> and <u>'s</u>, giving sentences like <u>I've been
here for hours</u> and <u>He's gone home already</u>. In Negro dialect,
the contracted forms <u>'ve</u> and <u>'s</u> can be removed, giving <u>I been
here for hours</u> and <u>He gone home already</u>. Rules for removing
the remnants of contraction account for at least three of the
most noticed features of Negro dialect, as we shall see. The
frequent operation of this rule, together with the relatively
infrequent use of the present perfective tense can lead to the
conclusion that <u>have</u> + past participle is not part of Negro
dialect. It is true that the present perfect tense is quite
infrequent. But the past perfect construction with <u>had</u> is,
if anything, even more common in Negro dialect narratives than
in narratives by speakers of standard American English. Sentences like <u>He had found the money</u> appear strikingly often in
story-telling. Negro dialect speakers do not select the
present perfect as often as do speakers of standard English,
but they select the past perfect more often than standard
English speakers. As with the -<u>ed</u> suffix, pronunciation rules
have removed forms which are present grammatically.
    3. <u>The past participle</u>. While it is quite clear that
the tenses formed grammatically with <u>have</u> and <u>had</u> are part of

Negro dialect, it is less clear whether or not there are past
participles in its grammar. In standard English, most past
participles are formed with the -ed suffix and so are identical with the past tense form. But there are a number of semi-
regular and irregular verbs for which the past participle and
past tense are formally distinguished (e.g. came versus has
come; ate versus has eaten, etc.). In Negro dialect, however,
it seems that there may not be any irregular verbs for which
the past tense and past participle are distinct. Sometimes
the standard English past participle form is generalized to
serve both functions (He taken it; He have taken it), but more
commonly the simple past form is used in both kinds of constructions (e.g. He came; He have came). For a few verbs,
some Negro dialect speakers generalize one form while others
generalize the other (e.g. He done it; He have done it; He
did it; He have did it). It is possible, then, that the Negro
dialect equivalents of the present and past perfect tenses are
not formed with forms of have plus the past participle, but
rather with a form of have plus a general past form.

    4. The completive aspect with done. Where standard
American English has only two aspectual contrasts of the perfective type, Negro dialect has four. With standard English,
Negro dialect has perfective tense (or aspect) constructions
with have and had. In addition, Negro dialect has a comple-
tive construction and a remote time construction. The com-
pletive aspect is formed from the verb done plus a past form
of the verb. Because of the uncertain status of the past
participle in the grammar of the dialect, it is difficult to
determine whether this form is the past participle or not.
This construction occurs in sentences like I done tried hard
all I know how and I done forgot what you call it.

    5. The remote time construction with been. A similar
construction with been indicates that the speaker conceives
of the action as having taken place in the distant past. The

remote aspect is used in <u>I been had it there for about three</u> <u>or four years</u> and <u>You won't get your dues that you been paid.</u> Often, the <u>been</u> construction is used with emphatic stress to doubly emphasize the total completion of an action, although it is not always used in this way. Unlike the <u>done</u> construction, the <u>been</u> construction is used only in Negro dialect. Both constructions are rather rare, at least in Northern cities.

The Third Person Singular Present Tense Marker

1. <u>General</u>. In standard American English, the suffix -<u>s</u> (or -<u>es</u>) is used to identify the present tense of a verb if the subject of that verb is in the third person singular. The paradigm is:

Singular	Plural
I walk	we walk
you walk	you walk
he walks; the man walks	they walk; the men walk

In a sense, the use of the -<u>s</u> suffix to mark present tense with third person singular subjects is an irregularity, since no suffix is used to mark present tense with other persons. The paradigm in Negro dialect is more regular:

Singular	Plural
I walk	we walk
you walk	you walk
he walk; the man walk	they walk; the men walk

It is important to realize that the -<u>s</u> suffix is not carelessly "left off" by speakers of Negro dialect. This suffix is simply not part of the grammar of the dialect.

2. <u>Auxiliary don't</u>. The verb <u>do</u> is used as an auxiliary in negative and other kinds of sentences. In Negro dialect, the -<u>s</u> suffix is absent from the auxiliary <u>don't</u> in the present tense when the subject is in the third person singular, just as it is from other third person singular present tense verbs. The equivalent of the standard English sentence <u>He doesn't go</u>,

then, is He don't go. Some other nonstandard dialects of English lack the -s suffix only with auxiliary don't. Speakers of such dialects rarely or never use sentences like He walk, but frequently use such sentences as He don't walk. The use of don't for doesn't in Negro dialect does not apply only to auxiliary don't, but is part of a general pattern involving all present tense verbs with subjects in the third person singular.[9]

3. Have and do. The verb have in standard English is unique in that the combination of have and the -s suffix results in has rather than haves. Similarly, when the -s suffix is added to do, the vowel quality changes and the result is does, not dos. Since the -s suffix does not exist in the verb system of Negro dialect, the verbs remain have and do with third person singular subjects in the present tense. For this reason, we observe sentences like He have a bike, He always do silly things, and I don't know if he like you, but I think he do.

4. Hypercorrect forms. The absence of the -s suffix in Negro dialect causes a real language learning problem when Negro dialect speakers come in contact with standard English. They observe that speakers of standard English have a suffix -s on some present tense verbs. But the grammatical rules restricting its use to sentences with third person singular subjects is just like a rule in the grammar of a foreign language. Like a foreign language learner, Negro dialect speakers begin to use the feature, but do not restrict it according to the rules of the new dialect. The result is that the -s subject is sporadically used with present tense verbs with subjects other than third person singular. This accounts for sentences like I walks, you walks, the children walks, etc., as well as the appropriate standard English He walks. Occasionally, the suffix is also added to non-finite forms, giving sentences like They want to goes. No Negro dialect speakers,

however, add the -s suffix to all present tense verbs with
non-third person singular subjects.

The use of sentences like I walks has a quite different
status from the use of sentences like He walk. A speaker of
Negro dialect uses walk instead of walks with a subject like
he because this is the correct form according to the grammatical rules of his dialect. He uses walks with subjects
like I, not because this grammar calls for this form but because of a partial learning of the grammar rules of a different dialect.

Future

1. Gonna. A very frequent future indicator in Negro
dialect, as in other dialects of English, is the use of gonna.
The rule for deleting is and are (see below) operates very
frequently when gonna follows, giving sentences like He gonna
go and You gonna get in trouble. So rarely is a form of be
used with gonna that it may seem that gonna is not related to
standard English be going to, but is an auxiliary in its own
right. However, the behavior of gonna as compared with true
auxiliaries like can shows that this is not the case. In
questions and in abbreviated sentences, can and gonna function
quite differently (Can he go? but never Gonna he go?; He can
sing, I know he can but He gonna vote for you, I know he is,
not I know he gonna). As Labov and his associates have pointed
out, the phonetic form of gonna can be reduced in a number of
ways in Negro dialect which are different from its reductions
in standard English. When the subject of the sentence is I
in standard dialects of American English, gonna can be reduced
to ngna (I'ngna go). In Negro dialect, there are three reductions not possible in standard English, mana (I'mana go), mon
(I'mon go) and ma (I'ma go). When the subject is something
other than I, Negro dialect may give the reduced form gon (He
gon go).[10]

2. _Will_. The use of _will_ to indicate future time reference is also part of both Negro dialect and standard English. As in the case of _has_ and _have_, _will_ can be contracted (to _'ll_). This contracted form, like _'ve_ and _'s_, can be eliminated, as we have seen, especially if the next word begins with a labial consonant, as in _He miss you tomorrow_. This makes it appear that the future is sometimes indicated by the use of the main verb alone.

Invariant Be

1. _General_. When the verb _to be_ is used as a main verb in standard English, it appears as one of the five variant inflected forms _is_, _are_, _am_, _was_ or _were_, depending on the verb tense and the person and number of the subject. In Negro dialect, the form _be_ can be used as a main verb, regardless of the subject of the sentence as in _I be here this afternoon_ and _Sometime he be busy_. This use of invariant _be_ in Negro dialect has two explanations; deleted _will_ or _would_ and distributive _be_.

2. _Will be or would be_. Since _be_ begins with a labial consonant, the _'ll_ contraction of _will_ is often absent before _be_. This is fairly common in Negro dialect, but also happens occasionally in standard English, giving sentences like _He be here pretty soon_. The contracted form of _would_ is _'d_, which can merge with the _b_ of _be_ or be removed by the final _d_ elimination rule. This process is another source for invariant _be_ and is quite common in standard English as well. A sentence like _If you gave him a present he be happy_ is possible both in standard dialects and in Negro dialect.

It may seem that an intolerable number of ambiguous sentences would result from the removal of the remnants of contraction. But the context usually makes the intended meaning clear. The same sort of thing happens in standard English, not only in the occasional removal of _'ll_ and _'d_, but in the contraction of _'d_ of both _had_ and _would_. The sentence _He'd_

<u>come home</u> is ambiguous by itself. But in contexts like <u>He'd</u>
<u>come home before I got there</u> or <u>He'd come home if he could</u>,
the meaning is clear.

    3. <u>Distributive or non-tense be</u>. The other source for
invariant <u>be</u> is very different. This type of invariant <u>be</u>
occurs because <u>to be</u> is possible in Negro dialect without tense
specification with a meaning something like "object or event
distributed intermittently in time". This use of <u>be</u>, as in
<u>Sometime he be there and sometime he don't</u>, occurs only in
Negro dialect and is usually misunderstood by standard English speakers. It is common for standard English speakers to
take non-tense <u>be</u> as a deviant form of <u>am</u>, <u>is</u>, or <u>are</u>, when
in fact it contrasts with these forms. To say <u>I'm good</u> is to
assert a permanent quality of oneself. To say <u>I be good</u> means
that the speaker is good only intermittently. Unlike the cases
of invariant <u>be</u> which are derived from <u>will be</u> or <u>would be</u>,
non-tense <u>be</u> usage is highly stigmatized socially. Because
there are three sources for invariant <u>be</u> in Negro dialect, any
positive statement containing invariant <u>be</u> is potentially three-
ways ambiguous. In the sentence <u>If somebody hit him, Darryl be</u>
<u>mad</u>, if the use of <u>be</u> is taken as coming from <u>would be</u>, it is a
hypothesis about how Darryl might act if he were hit. If <u>will</u>
<u>be</u> is understood, it is a prediction as to how Darryl will re-
act. If distributive <u>be</u> is the interpretation, it is a statement of Darryl's reaction to a certain kind of intermittent
event. The sentence is only ambiguous because it is a positive statement. In negative sentences, contraction of <u>will</u>
and <u>would</u> is not possible. The three interpretations above
would each be denied in a different way. The hypothesis
would be denied by <u>Darryl wouldn't be mad</u>, the predication
by <u>Darryl won't be mad</u>, and the statement by <u>Darryl don't</u>
<u>be mad</u>.

<u>Absence of Forms of To Be</u>

    1. <u>General</u>. When the <u>is</u> or <u>are</u> forms of <u>to be</u> are ex-
pected in standard English, Negro dialect may have no form at

all. When the subject is I, and the expected standard English
form is am, however, am or its contraction 'm is almost always
present. For most varieties of Negro dialect, the absence of
forms of to be represents the elimination of the contracted
forms 's and 're of is and are, much as the contractions of
have, has, will and would are removed. Just as in these cases
and in the case of the -ed suffix, the to be forms are grammatically present and are known to the speaker, but have been
removed by a pronunciation rule. It is not necessary to teach
the present tense forms of to be to speakers of Negro dialect,
but they will need to learn to contract these forms without
also deleting the remnants of contraction.

    2. Is. As we have seen, the absence of is is common
before gonna. Some Southern dialects of English besides Negro
dialect show the absence of is in this context. In Negro dialect, unlike other English dialects, is can be absent wherever
it can be contracted in standard English. We observe sentences like He a man, He running to school, That dude bad,
as well as He gonna go. When the subject of a sentence is
it, that, or what, the next word is is, an s-sound is usually
heard. This is not the 's from the contraction of is, however. The s in such sentences is the result of the following
process. First, is is contracted to 's. Then, the t of it,
that and what is transformed into s under the influence of
the 's from is. This leaves is's, thas's, and whas's. But
these forms are never heard because the 's from is is then
eliminated as it almost always must be when it follows a
sibilant. This leaves the pronunciations iss, thas and whas
for these three words. Apparently something similar happens
in the case of let's (pronounced les) even though the 's comes
from us rather than is.

    3. Are. The form are is present less often than the
form is in the speech of Negro dialect speakers. Are is also
absent in white Southern dialects of English which do not

allow the absence of is, including some which are socially
standard. The English contraction rule provides for the removal of all but the final consonant of certain auxiliaries
(are to 're, will to 'll, have to 've, etc.). In dialects
which lack r after most stressed vowels, are has no final
consonant (i.e. it is pronounced ah). Regular pronunciation
rules of English reduce this ah to uh. Applying the contraction rule to this pronunciation eliminates the word are
entirely, without utilizing the Negro dialect rule for removing the consonant. Because of this there are speakers who
have are absence but do not have is absence.

      4. Agreement with forms of to be. Some speakers show no
person-number agreement when full forms of to be are used.
The past tense form is was regardless of the subject, giving
sentences like They was there, You was there, etc. When the
full forms of the present tense form is used, is is used by
these speakers for all persons, e.g. The boys is there, You is
there, etc. However, some Southern speakers of Negro dialect
occasionally use are or even am as the general form of the
present tense of to be (There she are, You am a teacher, etc.).
NEGATION
The Use of Ain't
      Due to a series of phonetic changes in the history of Eng-
lish, the negative forms of is, are, am, and auxiliary have
and has became ain't. Although ain't is used by educated
speakers in casual conversation in some parts of the country,
the use of ain't in this way is one of the clearest and universal markers of nonstandard speech of all kinds. In some
varieties of Negro dialect, ain't also corresponds to standard
English didn't. This probably developed from rather recent
phonetic changes. In Negro dialect, negative forms of auxiliary
do can lose the initial d in casual speech. This gives, for
example, I 'on't know for standard English I don't know. In
the case of didn't, the second d can merge with the following n.

The result of these two developments is the pronunciation int
for didn't. This form is so similar in pronunciation and
function to the already existing ain't that the two forms
merged. For speakers of Negro dialect who have this use of
ain't, there are sentences like He ain't do it as well as
He ain't done it (or He ain't did it) and He ain't there.
The unfamiliarity of this usage to speakers of standard English often leads to misunderstanding between speakers of the
two dialects. A Negro dialect speaker may say He ain't touch
me which should be translated as He didn't touch me in standard English but be understood as having meant He hasn't touched
me (with the -ed suffix supplied by the hearer). Ain't is
often used with multiple negation, leading to sentences like
He ain't nobody, He ain't did nothing and He aint' go nowhere.

Multiple Negation

1. General. "Double negatives" or, more accurately,
multiple negation is another very common feature of nonstandard
dialects. A frequent misconception about multiple negation is
that it leads to misunderstanding because "two negatives make
a positive". For example, it is often said of a sentence like
He doesn't know nothing that the intention of the speaker is
reversed because if he doesn't know nothing, he must know
something. But in actual usage, sentences with multiple negatives are always understood as the speaker intends them, by
other speakers of nonstandard English and usually by speakers
of the standard dialects as well. The reason is that there is
basically only one negative in He doesn't know nothing which
is expressed in more than one place in the sentence. Standard
English allows negatives to be expressed only once; nonstandard
dialects have no such restriction. Yet there are strict grammar rules in nonstandard dialects of English which govern precisely at which places in a sentence a negative can be expressed.

2. Three negative placement rules in standard English.
To understand these facts, it is necessary to introduce a new

concept of grammar rule. We will conceive of all sentences
as starting out at an abstract level with an abstract structure which is not actually pronounced. What grammar rules do
is to take this unpronounceable abstract structure and convert
it, step by step, into an ordinary sentence which can actually
be spoken. These rules are partly the same for all dialects
of English, but partly different. These differences account
for the fact that the same basic structure can be expressed in
different ways in different dialects.

As an example, we will see what happens when the abstract
structure of the sentence Nobody knows anything is operated on
by the rules of standard English. At the abstract level, we
can think of the structure of Nobody knows anything as:
NOT+ANY-BODY+DOE-S+KNOW+ANY-THING. The element NOT is to be
understood as denying the truth value of the rest of the sentence. All dialects of English have a rule which requires
that this NOT be placed into any noun phrase containing the
indefinite element ANY, if that noun phrase comes before the
main verb. Because of this rule, the first rule of negative
placement, there are no dialects of English which have such
sentences as Anybody doesn't know anything or Anybody knows
nothing. We can symbolize the fact that NOT has been incorporated into ANY by changing the first plus sign to a dash.
This means that the element NOT is now part of the same word
as ANYBODY. The result is: NOT-ANY-BODY+DOE-S+KNOW+ANY-THING.
Since standard English allows the basic negative element NOT
to be expressed only once, this is the only negative placement rule which can be applied to this sentence. Later on,
there will be a rule to convert cases of NOT-ANY into no.
There is another rule which removes DO in sentences like this
one and attaches the -S to main verbs like KNOW. The final
result is Nobody knows anything.

In the sentence He doesn't know anything, there is no ANY
in the noun phrase which comes before the verb. The abstract

structure would be NOT+HE+DOE-S+KNOW+ANY-THING. Because there
is no ANY before the verb, the first negative placement rule
does not operate. NOT must be placed by the second negative
placement rule in this sentence. This rule stipulates that
the element NOT will be attached to the main verb phrase, if
the first rule is not applicable. The effect on our abstract
structure is: HE+DOE-S+NOT+KNOW+ANY-THING. There is a later
rule which contracts does not, giving doesn't.

In formal styles of standard English speech, it is possible to use sentences such as He knows nothing. This sentence results from the third negative placement rule, which
may be applied, but is not required. This rule allows a negative to be removed from the main verb phrase and be attached
to the first ANY which follows the verb phrase. This rule
operates on the result of the second negative placement rule.
As we know, the structure which results from the application
of this rule is HE+DOE-S+NOT+KNOW+ANY-THING. If the third
negative placement rule is selected, the structure of
HE+DOE-S+NOT+KNOW+ANY-THING is converted to HE+DOE-S+KNOW+
NOT-ANY-THING. After the rules for removing DO and converting
NOT-ANY to NO have been applied, HE+DOE-S+KNOW+NOT-ANY-THING
becomes He knows nothing.

3. The three negative placement rules in nonstandard
English. In standard English, the three negative placement
rules operate under the general restriction that the negative
element NOT can be expressed in the final version of any sentence only once. If the first rule applied, the second and
third rules do not. If the conditions for the use of the first
rule are not met, the second rule applies. In some styles of
speech, it is possible to use the third rule, but if it is used,
NOT is removed from the position given it by the second rule.
In nonstandard dialects, the second and third rules are copying
rules, not placement rules in the strictest sense. These rules
make a copy of the original NOT somewhere else in the sentence,

but leave the first NOT in its original position. Let us
examine the abstract structure NOT+ANY-BODY+DOE-S+KNOW+IT,
which would be expressed in standard dialects as <u>Nobody knows
it</u>. The first negative placement rule, as we have seen, operates in all dialects of English. In any variety of English,
the result of the first rule is NOT-ANY-BODY+DOE-S+KNOW+IT.
In standard English, the second and third rules are not allowed
to operate if the first rule has been applied. In some kinds
of nonstandard English, including Negro dialect, the second
negative placement rule is allowed to apply to NOT-ANY-BODY+
DOE-S+KNOW+IT as a copying rule. That is, it makes a copy of
NOT in the main verb phrase of the sentence, but leaves the
original NOT where it is. The result is: NOT-ANY-BODY+DOE-S+
NOT+KNOW+IT. When the rules which convert NOT-ANY to <u>no</u> and
contract <u>not</u> have been applied, the sentence comes out as
<u>Nobody doesn't know it</u>.[11] At this point it is essential to
keep in mind that <u>Nobody doesn't know it</u> comes from exactly the
same abstract structure as the standard English <u>Nobody knows
it</u> and means the same thing. The <u>n't</u> of <u>doesn't</u> is a mere
copy of the <u>no</u> of <u>nobody</u>. Unlike most kinds of multiple negation, sentences to which both the first and second rules have
been applied are likely to be misunderstood by speakers of
standard English. Standard English speakers would not expect
<u>Nobody doesn't know it</u> to have a negative meaning.

The third negative placement rule operates differently
in nonstandard dialects from the way in which it operates in
standard dialects. Like the nonstandard use of the second
rule above, the third rule in nonstandard English acts as a
copying rule. Consider the following structures: NOT+ANY-
BODY+DOE-S+KNOW+ANY-THING+ABOUT+ANY-THING (the basis for
standard English <u>Nobody knows anything about anything</u>), and
NOT+HE+DOE-S+KNOW+ANY-THING+ABOUT+ANY-THING (the basis for
standard English <u>He doesn't know anything about anything</u> or
<u>He knows nothing about anything</u>). The first negative placement

rule converts NOT+ANY-BODY+DOE-S+KNOW+ANY-THING+ABOUT+ANY-THING
to NOT-ANY-BODY+DOE-S+KNOW+ANY-THING+ABOUT+ANY-THING, incorporating NOT into ANY-BODY. In standard English, the second
and third placement rules can never apply if the first rule
applies. We have seen that the second negative placement rule
can apply in some nonstandard dialects as a copying rule, even
if the first rule has already operated. In most nonstandard
dialects, whether or not the second rule is allowed to operate
as a copying rule, the third rule is allowed to operate as
such. In this form, the third rule stipulates that NOT may be
copied with every ANY in the sentence, but also must be left
in its original position. When this rule applies in these
nonstandard dialects, it converts NOT-ANY-BODY+DOE-S+KNOW+
ANY-THING to NOT-ANY-BODY+DOE-S+KNOW+NOT-ANY-THING+ABOUT+NOT-
ANY-THING. After the rule about NOT-ANY and the rule about
DOES have operated, the result is: Nobody knows nothing about
nothing. Again it is imperative to keep in mind that the sentences Nobody knows anything about anything, Nobody knows
nothing about nothing and Nobody doesn't know nothing about
nothing are all equivalent in meaning. The multiple negative
expressions are simply different ways of copying the one basic
sentence-negating NOT.

If we take the structure, NOT+HE+DOE-S+KNOW+ANY-THING+
ABOUT+ANY-THING, we notice that the first rule does not apply,
since the first noun phrase does not contain ANY. If the first
rule does not apply, all dialects of English require that the
second rule apply, which places the NOT in the main verb
phrase. The result is HE+DOE-S+NOT+KNOW+ANY-THING+ABOUT+
ANY-THING. The third negative placement rule can apply, but
does not necessarily have to, in standard English. If it does
apply, it removes the NOT from the verb phrase and attaches it
to the first ANY. The ultimate result is He knows nothing
about anything. In nonstandard dialects, there are two differences. First, the rule is a copying rule, so the original

NOT remains in the main verb phrase. Furthermore, the NOT is copied with every ANY in the sentence, so that the resulting structure is HE+DOE-S+NOT+KNOW+NOT-ANY-THING+ABOUT+NOT-ANY-THING, and the ultimate sentence is He doesn't know nothing about nothing.

For some speakers of Negro dialect, the third rule must apply to every sentence with ANY after the main verb phrase. For these speakers, there are no such sentences as Nobody knows anything about anything and He doesn't know anything about anything; the grammar of this variety requires Nobody knows nothing about nothing and He doesn't know nothing about nothing. Another way of putting it is that the word any can never appear in the spoken form of a negative sentence.

4. Multiple negation in two clauses. The nonstandard applications of the second and third negative placement rules above only apply within a single clause. There is another type of multiple negation, which is possible for some Negro dialect speakers, in which negation may be marked in two different clauses. These speakers use sentences like Nobody didn't know it didn't rain meaning Nobody knew it rained. But such sentences are extremely rare.

5. Multiple negation with negative adverbs. Negation can be expressed with negative adverbs, as well as in verb phrases and by incorporation into ANY. Multiple negation can be expressed by a negative adverb and also by one of these other methods in the same sentence. The result is the utterance of sentences like He doesn't hardly come to see us any more, or more commonly, He doesn't come to see us any more, hardly. Standard English speakers who never use other kinds of multiple negation sometimes use sentences like the above. In Negro dialect, the marking of negation in the verb phrase or with ANY in sentences which contain hardly is the rule rather than the exception. Negro dialect, along with other nonstandard English dialects, also allows negation to be

multiply expressed when the same sentence contains the adverbs
never and neither.

6. Negativized auxiliary pre-position. If a sentence
has an indefinite noun phrase containing a negative marker
(nobody, nothing, no dog) before the verb, the negativized
form of the verbal auxiliary (can't, wasn't, didn't) may be
placed at the beginning of the sentence. The result is sentences like Can't nobody do it, Wasn't nothing wrong, and
Didn't no dog bite him. Although these sentences appear to
be questions in their written form, the intonation of the
spoken form in Negro dialect makes it clear that they are
statements. If the noun phrase before the verb does not contain a negativized indefinite, pre-position of the auxiliary
is not possible, so that a sentence like Don't the man do it
will not occur as a statement.

-s SUFFIXES

Possessive

1. With common nouns. Where the 's possessive appears
in standard English, Negro dialect indicates possessive by the
order of the words. The phrase The boy hat corresponds to
The boy's hat in the standard dialect. In Northern urban
Negro dialect, apparently no one uses the zero form of the
possessive exclusively; it alternates with the 's form. In
Southern varieties of Negro dialect it seems possible to find
speakers who do not use 's for possessive at all. There is
some reason to believe that the presence of the 's possessive
suffix is more common at the end of a clause (i.e. in absolute
position, as in The hat is the boy('s) than in the attributive
possessive (The boy('s) hat). It has been claimed that the 's
in this situation is regularly present. However the absence
of the 's suffix in the absolute possessive suffix has been
observed with some frequency in the speech of Northern urban
Negro dialect speakers and has been found to be extremely common in Southern Negro dialect data. Pedagogically, it would

seem wise to deal with both kinds, but to emphasize the attributive construction.

2. With personal names. Because the position of the 's
possessive is somewhat unstable in the grammar of Negro dialect, some speakers use the 's suffix inappropriately with
personal names when attempting to speak standard English.
In standard English, of course, the rule is that the 's suffix is attached to the surname when the possessor is identified by his full name (Jack Johnson's car). Occasionally, a
Negro dialect speaker will attach the 's suffix to both names
(Jack's Johnson's car) or to the first name (Jack's Johnson
car). This feature is not part of the grammar of Negro dialect but is a hypercorrection in attempting to use standard
English (cf. the hypercorrections in connection with the -s
third person singular present tense marker on p. 64).

3. Mines. Some speakers of Negro dialect use the form
mines for mine in the absolute possessive construction (never
in the attributive construction) giving sentences like This
mines. This is a regularization in Negro dialect of the
absolute possessive form of the first person pronoun to conform to the other pronoun forms which end in s (his, hers,
its, yours, ours, theirs).

4. Undifferentiated pronouns. Some speakers of Negro
dialect use the standard English nominative or accusative
forms of personal pronouns for possession in attributive constructions (he book, him book, we book, etc.). This feature,
which is probably to be ascribed to the lingering influence
of the grammar of Caribbean Creole languages in Negro dialect,
is extremely rare in the North but apparently somewhat more
common in the speech of young children in the South.

Plural

1. Absence of the plural suffix. The -s (or -es) suffixes which mark most plurals in standard English are occasionally absent in the speech of Negro dialect speakers. This

results in sentences like <u>He took five book</u> and <u>The other</u>
<u>teacher, they'll yell at you</u>. The absence of the plural suf-
fix in Northern urban Negro dialect occurs considerably less
often than the absence of the possessive suffix and far less
than the absence of the third person singular present tense
marker.[12] There is no question that most Northern speakers
of Negro dialect have the use of the plural suffix as part of
their grammar. Much of the absence of the plural suffix is
due to a difference in the classification of certain nouns in
Negro dialect from standard English. A few nouns do not take
the plural suffix at all in standard English (<u>one sheep</u>, <u>two</u>
<u>sheep</u>). Words which are so classified in Negro dialect, but
which take the regular -<u>s</u> plural in standard English include
<u>cent</u>, <u>year</u>, and <u>movie</u>. It is possible that the absence of
the plural suffix in words like <u>cent</u> and <u>year</u> is because the
grammar of Negro dialect allows the optional absence of the
plural marker with nouns of measure. Such a rule is also
part of the grammar of a number of white regional dialects.
For some speakers of Southern Negro dialect, particularly
young children, the plural suffix is almost always absent and
may well not be part of the grammar of their dialect at all.
The occasional claim that the plural suffix may only be absent
when the plural noun is preceded by a quantifier (<u>two</u>, <u>several</u>,
etc.), and not otherwise, is invalid. There are a great many
examples of plural nouns not preceded by a quantifier which
lack the plural suffix.

   2. <u>Regular plurals with irregular nouns</u>. Some nouns in
standard English form plurals by a vowel change (<u>one foot</u>, <u>two</u>
<u>feet</u>), or with no suffix at all (<u>one deer</u>, <u>two deer</u>). For many
Negro dialect speakers, these nouns take the regular -<u>s</u> suffix
(<u>two foots</u>, <u>two deers</u>). This is another example of a classification difference between the two kinds of English.

   3. <u>Double plurals</u>. Where standard English forms plurals
irregularly, Negro dialect may add the -<u>s</u> suffix to the

irregular plural (peoples, childrens). A possible historical
reason relates to an earlier stage of Negro dialect in which
the plural category was not part of the grammar.[13] In learning standard English, speakers of the dialect tended to add
the -s suffix to words which were already pluralized in an
irregular way. These doubly pluralized words became fossil-
ized and are preserved to the present. Words most frequently
affected are childrens, peoples, and mens.

QUESTIONS

Inversion

The form which questions take in standard English depends
on whether the question is direct or indirect. If the question
is direct, word-order inversion takes place, but if the question is indirect, the basic word order is retained. Inversion
affects the questioned element, if any, and the verbal auxiliary or copula, transferring them to the beginning of the
sentence. The statement He went somewhere can be content-
questioned or yes-no-questioned. To form the content question, somewhere is replaced by where, the auxiliary did is
added and both are moved to the head of the sentence, giving
Where did he go. The yes-no question simply requires the in-
sertion of the auxiliary did and its transfer to the head of
the sentence, giving Did he go somewhere. The indirect question involves the transfer of the questioned element to the
head of the clause only. In the case of yes-no questions, if
or whether is used in the construction. Examples of the two
types of indirect questions corresponding to He went somewhere
would be I want to know where he went and I want to know if
(whether) he went somewhere. In Negro dialect spoken in the
North, the inverted form of the question is used for both
direct and indirect questions and the words if and whether
are not used to form indirect yes-no questions. The direct
questions for He went somewhere are the same as the standard
English examples given above. But the two indirect questions

would be <u>I want to know where did he go</u> and <u>I want to know did
he go somewhere</u>. The Negro dialect grammar rules for question
formation are more regular than the standard English rules,
since they apply in the same way to both kinds of questions.[14]
Some speakers, on the other hand, have the uninverted form for
direct questions, at least in content questions. These speakers use questions like <u>What that is</u>? and <u>Where the white cat
is</u>?.

A historical process something like the following may
explain this state of affairs. The uninverted construction
is probably the older one. As Negro dialect began to approximate standard American English more closely, its speakers
noticed that the standard dialect had inverted direct questions. Since there was no distinction in Negro dialect between direct and indirect questions, inversion may have been
generalized to both types.

The Absence of Preposed Auxiliaries

In inverted direct questions, the auxiliary or copula
form of the main verb phrase is moved to the front of the sentence, as we have seen. In this position, some of these ele-
ments are especially vulnerable to deletion. This gives ques-
tions like <u>He coming with us</u>? (deletion of <u>is</u>), <u>Where you been</u>?
(deletion of <u>have</u>), and <u>You understand</u>? (deletion of <u>do</u>). Although this is frequently cited as a feature of nonstandard
dialects, deletion of these auxiliaries in direct questions
is very common in spoken standard English. Therefore, attempting to eliminate this kind of auxiliary deletion from the
speech of inner-city Negro children would be a low-priority
task.

PRONOUNS

A number of usages involving personal, demonstrative and
relative pronouns are sometimes cited as examples of non-
standard dialect usage. We will discuss only two of them
here.

Pronominal Apposition

A well-known, but little understood feature of nonstandard English dialects including Negro dialect, is pronominal apposition. Pronominal apposition is the construction in which a pronoun is used in apposition to the noun subject of the sentence. Usually the nominative form of the pronoun is used, as in My brother, he bigger than you or That teacher, she yell at the kids all the time. Occasionally, the objective or possessive pronoun is used in apposition as well, as in That girl name Wanda, I never did like her or Mr. Smith, I got one F in his class one time. It was discovered in a study of Detroit speech that pronominal apposition was used by all speakers whether they were speakers of standard English or not. It seems likely that the length of the modifying material which intervenes between the noun and the pronoun has an effect on acceptability; the more intervening material, the more acceptable the pronoun in apposition. For example, pronominal apposition in a sentence like That man that I met on the train to Chicago last week, he turned out to be a Congressman is more acceptable than in a sentence such as My mother, she's here now.[15] But the exact restrictions on the acceptable usage of pronominal apposition have yet to be discovered. Negro dialect speakers who use the stigmatized kinds of pronominal apposition do not use it in every sentence. It has been suggested that the use of pronominal apposition is related to the entry and re-entry of participants in a narrative, but this hypothesis has not been thoroughly investigated.

Existential It

Where standard English uses there in an existential or expletive function, Negro dialect has it. This results in sentences like It's a boy in my room name Robert and Is it a Main Street in this town? where standard English would have There's a boy ... and Is there a Main Street .... This difference in the choice of one word in a single construction,

affects the understanding of a considerable number of sentences
in ordinary speech. For example, a television advertisement
for a brand of powdered soup contained the line Is it soup yet?
This was intended to mean something like Has it become soup
yet? and was no doubt so understood by the standard English
speaking audience, except possibly in parts of the South.
But speakers of Negro dialect might well understand the same
sentence as something like Is there any soup yet?

CONCLUSION

It should be clear from our approach to the features discussed here that we are not using the terms "grammar rule" and
"pronunciation rule" in the traditional sense. As in the physi-
cal sciences, in which laws are discovered by observing natural
phenomena and are not imposed on nature by scientists, so grammar rules and pronunciation rules are discovered by observing
actual usage rather than taken as given and imposed on people's
speech. For this reason, we can speak meaningfully of the
grammar and pronunciation rules of a nonstandard dialect. For
this reason also, some of the rules cited for standard American
English will appear startling. In both cases, the rules are
discovered from careful observation of usage. It is proper to
refer to "rules" because in no speech (except possibly in the
speech of the mentally ill or brain-damaged) are words randomly
put together. Negro dialect and other nonstandard linguistic
systems operate under rules just as do socially favored dialects. But the rules are different.

Because this is the nature of the rules of language, it
is therefore important to uphold real spoken standard English
as a model to inner-city children rather than an artificially
precise language based on an arbitrary prescriptive norm of
what is "correct". A good rule of thumb for a teacher to
follow is to carefully and honestly reflect on his own usage
in casual conversation and not to insist on any usage on the
part of his pupils which he does not find in his own casual

speech. Children, and perhaps especially Negro children, are quick to detect hypocrisy and will soon lose all motivation if they see that they are being taught "better" English than their teacher actually uses himself.

The grammatical aspects of Negro dialect which have been outlined here are by no means the only ones which differ from standard American English. Yet, we have said something about all the most crucial features. Hopefully, an accurate understanding of some of the grammar of the dialect will contribute to the more efficient teaching of standard American English as an alternative way of speaking.

NOTES

1. We will assume throughout this article that the question of whether or not there is such a thing as "Negro dialect" distinct from white nonstandard dialects has been answered in the affirmative. Discussion of this issue is to be found in any of the articles by William A. Stewart listed in the bibliography. The use here of the term "Negro dialect" is equivalent to our use of "Black English" elsewhere and approximately equivalent to the use of "Negro Non-Standard English" by others. Unfortunately, there is no consensus about an adequate label for this variety of English, so that we have adopted the more traditional term.

2. "Consonant blends" is sometimes used by educators where we have used consonant clusters, but the meaning is the same.

3. "Base word" refers to the part of the word to which inflections may be added. For example, in the words drowned and drowns, drown is considered the base part of the word.

4.` The rules which govern standard English as it is actually spoken are often quite different from the prescriptive norms that are set up in school grammar textbooks.

5. In standard English, these sequences are often pronounced by lengthening the s instead of pronouncing the full sequence (e.g. tess for tests or dess for desks).

6. In some parts of the South t or d occurs at the end of the word in Negro dialect, regardless of what precedes th. Thus we may get toot or Rut' for tooth and Ruth.

7. There are, however, two exceptions. Some verbs, like
   berate, end in t or d followed by "silent e". When -ed
   (actually only d) is added to these verbs, the pronunciation is still id. In the second case, English has a set
   of verbs ("strong verbs") like hit and cost, which never
   take the -ed suffix. All "strong verbs" end in t or d.

8. This seems to be a different rule from the d-elimination
   rule discussed in the pronunciation section of this article

9. Teachers are sometimes doubly surprised when they hear
   sentences like He don't suppose to bring his books to
   class. Not only is the -s suffix absent from auxiliary
   don't, but the presence of don't instead of a form of to be
   is strikingly different from standard English. In Negro
   dialect, the word is not the participle supposed, but is a
   verb suppose which functions grammatically like the verb
   intend. Thus we get He don't suppose to bring... parallel
   with He don't intend to bring....

10. It is difficult to indicate the pronunciations intended by
    the spellings mon and gon. The on in each case is to be
    taken as a nasalized o-like vowel (giving [mõ] and [gõ]).

11. In Negro dialect, of course, the third person singular -s
    suffix would ordinarily not be present and this sentence
    would be Nobody don't know it. For simplicity in com-
    paring standard and nonstandard sentences, we will ignore
    this fact.

12. This was true of studies in New York, Detroit, and Wash-
    ington, D.C.

13. This statement is not to be taken as implying that Negro
    dialect at this or any other stage is a cognitively
    deficient system. Many languages in which there is an
    abundance of philosophical and literary works, like
    Chinese, also lack plural as a grammatical category.

14. There seems to be some evidence that this regularization
    is coming into standard English, since sentences like the
    last two are sometimes heard in the standard dialects.

15. Fasold once tested the sentence That man that I met on the
    train to Chicago last week, he turned out to be a Congress-
    man for acceptability with a class of university graduate
    students and none found it ungrammatical.

BIBLIOGRAPHY

Non-Technical Descriptions

BARATZ, JOAN C. 1969. "Teaching Reading in an Urban Negro
School System", Teaching Black Children to Read, ed. by Joan C.
Baratz and Roger W. Shuy, 92-116. Washington, D.C.: Center for
Applied Linguistics.
   Presents arguments, backed by experimental evidence, that
Negro dialect is a different, but not deficient, kind of Eng-
lish from standard English and suggests implications for read-
ing education.

STEWART, WILLIAM A. 1967. "Sociolinguistic Factors in the
History of American Negro Dialects", The Florida FL Reporter
5:2.11, 22, 24, 26.

-----. 1968. "Continuity and Change in American Negro Dialects", The Florida FL Reporter 6:1.3-4, 14-16, 18.
   These two articles outline the historical development of
Negro dialect and give examples of modern survivals from a
putative early slave Creole language.

-----. 1969. "On the Use of Negro Dialect in the Teaching of
Reading", Teaching Black Children to Read, ed. by Joan C.
Baratz and Roger W. Shuy, 156-219. Washington, D.C.: Center
for Applied Linguistics.
   Proposes that Negro dialect texts be used in reading education and outlines the language interference problems which
make this necessary.

WOLFRAM, WALTER A. and RALPH W. FASOLD. 1969. "Toward Reading Materials for Speakers of Black English: Three Linguistically Appropriate Passages", Teaching Black Children to Read,
ed. by Joan C. Baratz and Roger W. Shuy, 138-155. Washington,
D.C.: Center for Applied Linguistics.
   A discussion of the use of Negro dialect reading materials
including three sample passages with annotations to the grammatical features they contain.

Technical Descriptions

FASOLD, RALPH W. 1969. "Tense and the Form Be in Black English", Language 45:763-776.
   A technical analysis of the use of one feature, invariant
be, in Negro dialect.

LABOV, WILLIAM. 1966. The Social Stratification of English
in New York City. Washington, D.C.: Center for Applied Linguistics.
   A broad, detailed analysis of the social and linguistic

factors which affect several pronunciation features in New
York City speech. Not limited to Negro dialect.

------. 1969. "Contraction, Deletion and Inherent Variability
of the English Copula", Language 45:715-762.
    A technical analysis of the absence of forms of to be in
Negro dialect with implications for linguistic theory.

LABOV, WILLIAM, PAUL COHEN, CLARENCE ROBINS and JOHN LEWIS.
1968. A Study of the Non-Standard English of Negro and Puerto
Rican Speakers in New York City. Volume I: Phonological and
Grammatical Analysis. Final Report, Cooperative Research
Project No. 3288, U.S. Office of Education.
    Probably the most comprehensive linguistic and social analysis
of Negro speech in existence. Based on the speech of teen-age
peer groups from Harlem.

SHUY, ROGER W., WALTER A. WOLFRAM and WILLIAM K. RILEY. 1967.
Linguistic Correlates of Social Stratification in Detroit
Speech. Final Report, Cooperative Research Project No. 6-1347,
U.S. Office of Education.
    Preliminary social and linguistic analysis of several speech
features of Detroit speakers of both races.

WOLFRAM, WALTER A. 1969. A Sociolinguistic Description of
Detroit Negro Speech. Washington, D.C.: Center for Applied
Linguistics.
    A technical linguistic and social analysis of several of
the most important grammatical and pronunciation features in
Negro speech in a large metropolitan center.

THE USE OF NONSTANDARD ENGLISH IN

TEACHING STANDARD: CONTRAST AND COMPARISON

by Irwin Feigenbaum

In the past few years, there has been an increase in the
attention given to nonstandard dialects of English and to
teaching the standard dialect in our schools. One methodology
that has held some promise is that of teaching standard English as a second dialect in the way that English is taught as
a second language. This has several labels, among which are
"the aural-oral approach", "the linguistic method", "the
audio-lingual method", and "pattern practice". Using this
approach raises some questions about the place of a given
nonstandard dialect in teaching standard English to the
speakers of that dialect: Is the nonstandard a valid linguistic system that should be recognized and utilized in classroom instruction and/or in the development of pedagogical
materials? If it is used, how can it be made an effective
part of the instruction and not simply an interesting decor-
ation?

The Relative Values of Two Dialects: Appropriateness

"We should avoid the use of nonstandard English in the
classroom; it reinforces wrong English." This statement expresses one of the strongest and most common objections to
the use of nonstandard in teaching standard English. It is
felt that "wrong English" in the classroom will decrease the
quality of the instruction. But what is meant by the term
"wrong English?" It probably means "wrong standard English",
for, although the sentence He work hard. is incorrect standard
English, it is a correct nonstandard English sentence. Similarly, He works hard. is incorrect in nonstandard but correct

in standard. We are dealing with two separate dialects. One
of them is the standard. The other is different from the
standard.

The term "different" does not mean "right" or "wrong".
There are no linguistic criteria by which a given language or
dialect of a language can be proven "more wrong" than another.
Linguistics does not provide a means for determining the
intrinsic "rightness" or sophistication of a linguistic system.
Languages have order; they are systematic; and it is impossible to find criteria for determining the relative values of
two systems.[1] This does not imply that any language is as good
or useful as any other in every situation. What this does
mean is that, linguistically, no language system can be proven
more or less valid than another.

There is a criterion, however, for selecting one language
or dialect for use in a given situation; that criterion is
"appropriateness". This can be illustrated with an example
using foreign languages. In France, the language of govern-
mental activities is French. It is French not because of
some linguistic property of the French language but because
of its appropriateness. The appropriate language or dialect
can be determined negatively, by eliminating the inappropriate
ones. To determine appropriateness, we ask the following
questions: Is the variety of language used appropriate to the
social situation in which it is used? Does this variety call
the least attention to itself when it is used in the given
social situation?[2] French is appropriate in the situation described above; other languages are inappropriate. English, for
example, would be inappropriate because it would not be generally understood and people would be aware of the language
spoken instead of what is said in that language. The relative
value of French vis-a-vis English is not based on a linguistic criterion but on a social one. French is not intrinsically better or worse than English; however, for a given situation, one but not the other may be appropriate.

We find a similar situation with standard English and a nonstandard dialect. There is no criterion for proving the linguistic superiority of one of the dialects, and, as in the case of French and English described above, there are situations in which nonstandard English may be appropriate and situations in which standard English may be appropriate. In class, standard English is appropriate. In the cafeteria or at a basketball game, a group of students may find nonstandard appropriate. Appropriateness varies with the place and the participants in the conversation. A language variety that is appropriate in one social situation may not be appropriate in another.

Because there are situations in which nonstandard is appropriate, it would be unwise to eradicate it in teaching standard English. Our objective is to provide the students with this other variety of language, so that their linguistic behavior can be appropriate when the situation requires standard English. Even if it were possible to "stamp out" nonstandard English, changing the students' language behavior completely might be detrimental to their social well-being. They may need the nonstandard for social situations in which it is appropriate.

It is reasonable to say that there are many ways of speaking English, that there are social and geographical variations within English, and that speaking a nonstandard dialect does not indicate laziness or stupidity. A teacher can make these points in the classroom without decreasing the quality of the instruction. On the contrary, discussing these ideas can be beneficial, for the students are aware of the social uses of language, both their own and others.[3] Stating the truth will establish a better rapport between the teacher and the students, and it will help in enlisting their cooperation in the learning task. Common sense is one of the best -- and easiest -- ways of motivating.

There is a lot to be gained by acknowledging the existence of nonstandard English as a legitimate linguistic system. The approach to the students can be direct. The
inclusion of nonstandard may make the task more interesting
because the students have the opportunity to investigate a
portion of their own behavior, furnishing language data which
they are in a special position to provide. If they understand
the regularity of their own language, they may find it easier
to comprehend the systematic differences between nonstandard
and standard, since the differences will not be random.

Contrast and Comparison: Describing the Problems

Nonstandard English is useful in determining the standard English features that must be taught and those that need
not be, and in pointing out the differences between the standard English constructions to be taught and the equivalent or
close nonstandard ones. This is done through a technique from
second language pedagogy, contrastive linguistics. In foreign
language instruction, the difficult learning areas, as well as
the areas of little or no difficulty, are determined by contrasting the grammatical and phonological systems of the
student's native language with the systems of the language to
be learned.

If the target language is French and the student's native
language is English, the teacher and the materials writer know
the following:

(1)   There will be no problem when the student uses his Eng-
      list [d] in French words containing the similar French
      sound.

(2)   The student will have some difficulty in distinguishing
      the French [t] and [d] at the beginning of words because,
      in English, he is accustomed to an additional clue --
      aspiration -- found in English [t^huw] but not in [duw].

(3)   The student will need extensive work on the different
      forms of French adjectives. English has one form good;

French has four: <u>bon livre</u>; <u>bonne amie</u>; <u>bons élèves</u>; and <u>bonnes âmes</u>.

With the prediction of problem and non-problem areas, our teaching can be efficient: teach the problems; avoid the non-problems.

A contrastive analysis of a nonstandard dialect found in Washington, D.C., and the standard variety found there would provide the following information:

(1) The students do not distinguish [ɪ] and [ɛ] before nasal consonants; for example, <u>pin</u> and <u>pen</u> sound alike. But, since many speakers of standard English in other parts of the United States do not distinguish them either, it may not be worth spending very much time teaching the difference.

(2) The students often use an [f] sound at the end of words like <u>mouth</u>. In nonstandard, <u>Ruth</u> and <u>roof</u> sound alike, but <u>fin</u> and <u>thin</u> do not.

(3) The nonstandard verb paradigm in the present tense has one form. The comparable paradigm in standard English has two forms: <u>work</u> and <u>works</u>. The problem is to teach the marking of verbs after <u>he</u>, <u>she</u>, <u>Paula</u>, etc., but to keep the students from generalizing to the paradigm <u>I works</u>, <u>you works</u>, <u>he works</u>.

By recognizing the existence and the legitimacy of nonstandard, the materials developer can prepare efficient lessons that deal with real problems, and the teacher can know more precisely what the students' learning problems are.

<u>Contrast and Comparison: Teaching the Problems</u>

By comparing the standard English structure to be taught and the equivalent or close nonstandard structure, the student can see how they differ. Many students have a partial knowledge of standard English, that is, they can recognize and produce it but without accurate control. The instruction should include practice in sorting out standard from non-

standard. This practice can be provided when both standard
and nonstandard are used in the class. For many other students, this sorting out is the beginning of a series of steps
from passive recognition to active production.

(A)   Presentation

One way in which the standard-nonstandard contrast can
be employed in the class is in presenting a lesson or an
exercise. Two items, one standard and the other nonstandard,
show the students the structure to be learned and practiced,
and indicate where mistakes may occur. For example, the following two sentences may be written on the board or projected
from a transparency:

He work hard.

He works hard.

The teacher would then ask how the two sentences differ and
which one is standard and which nonstandard.[4] The teacher may
wish to tell the class that the second sentence has an "s"
on works and the first does not and that the first sentence
is nonstandard and the second standard, but, since the students are aware of the social uses of language, they should
be able to provide the answers. Asking for their observations will make the activity more interesting.

The simple activity described above takes very little
time: probably not more than fifteen seconds. Yet, in this
short period of time, the students have sorted out and identified standard and nonstandard, and they have indicated the
particular feature that distinguishes nonstandard and standard English without an involved grammatical explanation.

(B)   Discrimination Drills

A discrimination drill gives the students practice in
discriminating between standard and nonstandard English on
the basis of the feature being worked on. In this type of
drill, pairs of sentences or words are presented to the students orally. The students indicate whether the two are the

same or different (this drill is also known as a "same/
different drill"). Drill #1 is an example of this drill-
type.

#1

Teacher stimulus	Student response
1. He work hard. He works hard.	1. different
2. He work hard. He work hard.	2. same
3. Paula likes leather coats. Paula likes leather coats.	3. same
4. She prefers movies. She prefer movies.	4. different
5. Robert play guard. Robert play guard.	5. same

In this drill, we make certain that the students can hear the
feature that distinguishes standard from nonstandard. The
only difference between the sentences in items 1 and 4 in
Drill #1 is the verb ending. If the students respond correctly to the five items in the drill, we know that their
attention has been directed to the feature and that they hear
it consistently.

(C) Identification Drills

A general principle in second-language pedagogy is that
production is easier for the students after they have learned
to discriminate and identify what they will be called on to
produce. The identification drill contributes to this pre-
production work. This drill is more difficult than the discrimination drill in that the students are not presented with
material to compare but are required to identify a single
word or sentence without the assistance of a second item.
In Drill #2, the identification is "standard" or "nonstandard".[5]

#2

Teacher stimulus	Student response
1. He work hard.	1. nonstandard
2. He works hard.	2. standard
3. Paula likes leather coats.	3. standard
4. She prefer movies.	4. nonstandard
5. Paula likes leather coats.	5. standard
6. Robert play guard.	6. nonstandard
7. He drive a motorcycle.	7. nonstandard
8. Mr. Brown teaches geography.	8. standard
9. She ride on the bus.	9. nonstandard
10. Robert plays guard.	10. standard

In Drill #2, the only indication of "standard" or "nonstandard" is the verb ending. If the students respond correctly, we know that they can hear the feature that distinguishes standard from nonstandard English and that they can identify the two dialects on the basis of the feature.

(D) Translation Drills

In a translation drill the students translate a word or sentence from nonstandard to standard or from standard to nonstandard. Two short examples of this drill-type follow:

#3

Teacher stimulus	Student response
1. He works hard.	1. He work hard.
2. Paula likes leather coats.	2. Paula like leather coats.
3. She prefers movies.	3. She prefer movies.
4. Robert plays guard.	4. Robert play guard.
5. He drives a motorcycle.	5. He drive a motorcycle.

#4

Teacher stimulus	Student response
1. He work hard.	1. He works hard.

2. Robert play guard.	2. Robert plays guard.
3. Mr. Brown teach English.	3. Mr. Brown teaches English.
4. She ride on the bus.	4. She rides on the bus.
5. He prefer movies.	5. He prefers movies.

While keeping the students' attention focused on the feature in question, these exercises give them controlled practice in producing standard English. It is assumed that the students can produce nonstandard, and one may legitimately raise the objections that Drill #3 calls for the students to practice what they already can do and that producing nonstandard is not the objective of the instruction. This drill is useful in providing a further opportunity for the students to hear the standard forms they will be called on to produce, but, if this extra help seems unnecessary, Drill #4 may be used alone.

Drill #5 illustrates another format for translation drills.

#5

Teacher stimulus	Student response
1. He work hard.	1. He works hard.
2. He works hard.	2. He work hard.
3. Paula likes leather coats.	3. Paula like leather coats.
4. She prefer movies.	4. She prefers movies.
5. Paula likes leather coats.	5. Paula like leather coats.
6. Robert play guard.	6. Robert plays guard.
7. He drive a motorcycle.	7. He drives a motorcycle.
8. Mr. Brown teaches geography.	8. Mr. Brown teach geography.
9. She ride on the bus.	9. She rides on the bus.
10. Robert plays guard.	10. Robert play guard.

In this drill, the students make one overt response, but, in reality, they make two: the first is to identify the sentence

as standard or nonstandard; the second is to translate from
one to the other. This combination sub-type is more difficult than one in which the direction of translation is uniform. In some classes, it may be necessary to teach the
combination translation drill after the other two (thus presenting the tasks of identification and translation separately
before putting them together).[6] Some other classes may be
ready for the combination sub-type without the two preliminary
steps.

More complex translation drills can be constructed. In
Drills #6 and #7, the formats and directions of translation
are the same as in #3 and #4, respectively. The added complexity is the difference between the standard English verb
forms with he and they. Since this difference does not exist
in nonstandard, translation in either direction will be chal-
lenging (although the objections raised above still pertain).

#6

Teacher stimulus	Student response
1. He works hard.	1. He work hard.
2. They like nylon jackets.	2. They like nylon jackets.
3. She prefers movies.	3. She prefer movies.
4. The player works hard.	4. The player work hard.
5. The men drive fast.	5. The men drive fast.

#7

Teacher stimulus	Student response
1. He work hard.	1. He works hard.
2. They like nylon jackets.	2. They like nylon jackets.
3. She prefer movies.	3. She prefers movies.
4. The men drive too fast.	4. The men drive too fast.
5. The player work hard.	5. The player works hard.

One additional complication has appeared: it is impossible to
identify They work hard. as standard or nonstandard. This

point must be clear to the students so that they do not search for a differentiating feature. No major problems should occur in Drills #6 and #7 because the direction of translation is uniform. A drill like #8 is possible only if the students understand the status of a sentence like They work hard. and know how they are to respond to it in the drill.

#8

Teacher stimulus	Student response
1. He works hard.	1. He work hard.
2. He work hard.	2. He works hard.
3. They work hard.	3. They work hard.
4. Paula likes nylon jackets.	4. Paula like nylon jackets.
5. The lady teach history.	5. The lady teaches history.
6. The man drive a lot.	6. The man drives a lot.
7. The students ride on the bus.	7. The students ride on the bus.
8. The student ride on the bus.	8. The student rides on the bus.
9. Robert plays guard.	9. Robert play guard.
10. The ladies teach English.	10. The ladies teach English.

(E) Response Drills

The standard/nonstandard contrast and comparison can be carried into freer activities, in which the students have the opportunity of speaking more naturally. The drill-types described above provide very careful control of the linguistic material the students employ: their responses are predetermined at the textbook-writing stage. Other drill-types and activities have less control and give the students the chance to approach generating completely natural English. They still constrain the students' language but differently and less rigidly.

Drill #9 is one such drill-type (in this drill, the students are to contradict the statement with an appropriate

response -- standard statement and response or nonstandard
statement and response).

#9

Teacher stimulus	Student response
1. Your best friend work after school.	1. No, he don't.[7]
2. He gets good grades.	2. No, he doesn't.
3. The teacher doesn't give too much work.	3. Yes, she does.
4. His girlfriend chews gum all the time.	4. No, she doesn't.
5. Her boyfriend don't drive fast.	5. Yes, he do.
6. Your math teacher give good grades.	6. No, she don't.
7. The principal acts very friendly.	7. No, he doesn't.
8. She don't arrive late on Monday.	8. Yes, she do.
9. Your friend trust you with his car.	9. No, he don't.
10. William likes tall girls.	10. No, he doesn't.

In this drill, the student's attention is focused on the grammatical feature that marks standard and nonstandard. In addition, the student has an opportunity to respond more
naturally than in the previous drill-types, which involve
grammatical manipulation instead of conversation-like activity.
We make certain that the students' response will contain do or
does because of the statement to which they respond. The additional change -- negative to affirmative or affirmative to
negative -- provides a further challenge. However, if this
addition makes the drill too difficult, Drill #9 could be
replaced or preceded by two other drills. One of the drills
would require only affirmative responses and the other only
negative responses.

There can be a practically unlimited gradation within
the range of activities called "response drills". In #9, the

controls are still relatively tight. In Drill #10, they are
considerably more relaxed because, in answering the question
and adding another statement, the student is free to generate
his own material:

#10

1. Do his sister go to this school?

2. Does his sister go to this school?

3. Does a boa constructor crush its victims?

4. Do your brother get good grades?

5. Does he have a brother?

6. Does your English teacher give hard homework?

7. Does a rhinoceros have a trunk?

8. Do your aardvark like big ants?

9. Does your worst enemy like the zoo?

10. Do she go there often?

The standard/nonstandard difference is still at work. To this
has been added the choice of responses. The burden of speaking
appropriately is on the student. Drills #9 and #10 could be
made more natural and less controlled (and, consequently, more
difficult) by including sentences that have plural subjects.
Throughout the drills, as the controls are decreased, two objectives remain: distinguishing standard English from non-
standard and speaking accurate standard English when it is
appropriate.

The presentation statement and these drill-types are
ways in which nonstandard English can be used to make teaching standard English grammar more effective. They can be used
in teaching standard English pronunciation, too. Drills #11,
#12, and #13 deal with the pronunciation of the standard Eng-
lish final [θ] sound.[8]

#11

Teacher stimulus	Student response
1. mouth 'mouf'	1. different

2. mouth   2. same
    mouth

3. 'teef'   3. same
    'teef'

4. cloth   4. same
    cloth

5. 'clof'   5. different
    cloth

#12

Teacher stimulus   Student response

1. 'mouf'   1. nonstandard

2. mouth   2. standard

3. teeth   3. standard

4. 'teef'   4. nonstandard

5. cloth   5. standard

6. 'bof'   6. nonstandard

7. 'baf'   7. nonstandard

8. both   8. standard

9. 'clof'   9. nonstandard

10. bath   10. standard

#13

Teacher stimulus   Student response

1. 'mouf'   1. mouth

2. mouth   2. 'mouf'

3. teeth   3. 'teef'

4. 'teef'   4. teeth

5. cloth   5. 'clof'

6. 'bof'   6. both

7. 'baf'   7. bath

8. both   8. 'bof'

9. 'clof'   9. cloth

10. bath   10. 'baf'

Using the Drills in Class

These drills are oral drills, meant for oral presentation by the teacher and oral responses from the students.

Writing can be a valuable aid in making a point clear or as
a reminder on the board while the oral drill is in progress,
but, if the goal is control of oral standard English, the
instruction must provide as much practice in this medium as
possible. Drills of the type shown in this paper would be
conducted by the teacher, with no material for the individual
students. This allows maximum control of the students' attention: the teacher can regulate the amount of explanation, skip
over or repeat drills, and decide whether to introduce phonetic
symbology or unusual spellings.

The drills are of moderate intrinsic interest after the
initial novelty has worn off. One way to maintain interest
is in the pace of teaching them. A brisk, regular rhythm
works against the repetitiveness of drilling and the un-
naturalness of the responses. These drills are intended for
fast-paced instruction without lengthy accompanying explanations. The drilling is best conducted for brief periods of
time on a regular basis: ten to fifteen minutes a class period.

It is extremely important to use and require from the
students only completely natural standard English. The students are learning to recognize certain features in standard
and to produce standard. They are not aided by hearing exag-
gerated pronunciations and slow renditions because they will
not hear them in the real situations in which standard is
used. Demanding that students produce very precisely pronounced standard English does not help them speak a variety
that "calls the least attention to itself"; that is, a natural
standard.[9] There is another problem in using and requiring
hypercorrect language; this problem arises from the studens'
awareness of language and its social uses. As soon as a student realizes that he is being taught something false, he may
begin to reject the premise of appropriateness, on which
teaching standard English must be based.

Saying things naturally is applicable to the drills in
another way. Outside of the specific grammatical or phonological content of the drill, there should be no indication
of the response. It is very easy to let vocal intonation
indicate whether two items are the same or different. Some
teachers pause or slow down at the place in a sentence that
indicates "same/different" or "standard/nonstandard". If the
students are to respond accurately to normal standard, they
must hear it in the classroom.

Some teachers may feel uncomfortable about using non-
standard English in their classes. There seems to be a feeling that the written word or the teacher's spoken word is
extremely powerful and that it will have a deep and lasting
adverse effect on the student's use of English. How can
there be an adverse effect when a nonstandard word or sentence
will only show the students what they already know? Students
do not react strongly when they encounter a sentence like
He work hard., and, after the first momentary surprise at
seeing or hearing nonstandard in class, they accept it as a
natural part of the work.

There is a way to rescue the teacher who feels very uncomfortable about speaking nonstandard before the class: a
student can lead the drill. The other students will pay close
attention to what the student-leader says; the nonstandard
will sound more natural; and the added interest and variety
will make the exercise seem fun, with much of the drill-like
atmosphere gone.

Nonstandard English can be profitably utilized in the
pedagogy of standard English, both in materials development
and in classroom teaching. The drills and techniques discussed in this paper do not constitute an exhaustive listing,
and there is no implication that they are in themselves sufficient. There are effective drill-types in which only standard is used. The goal of the instruction is to teach a control

of oral standard English. Any drill or procedure which fur-
thers this goal without introducing extraneous diversions or
requiring a lot of time is worth trying.

NOTES

1. If, for example, one measured the inflectional complexity
    of their noun systems, Latin with its many case endings
    would rank higher than modern English. This does not,
    however, <u>prove</u> that Latin is better or more sophisticated
    than English because one could just as easily claim that
    a sophisticated language uses the device of word order to
    express what a less sophisticated language must express
    by word endings.

2. These two questions are taken from a discussion of
    "appropriateness" in Irwin Feigenbaum, "The Concept of
    Appropriateness and Developing Materials for TESOL",
    <u>TESOL Quarterly</u>, vol. 1, no. 3, September, 1967, pp. 36-
    39.

3. Throughout this paper the references will be to students
    in junior and senior high schools, with whom the author
    has worked; however, there may be applications to younger
    students as well.

4. The use of the identifying terms "standard" and "non-
    standard", "school English" and "out-of-school English",
    etc., presupposes some discussion about appropriateness,
    in which these terms were presented and defined.

5. The identification could be the presence or absence of
    "s" (or "es") in the written forms, but this difference
    may not be so real and important to the students as the
    difference between potentially appropriate and inappro-
    priate behavior.

6. The two steps in Drill #5 can be regarded as a combina-
    tion of Drill #2 (identification) and Drills #3 and #4
    (translation).

7. In a drill with several possible responses for each
    statement, the students should be called on individually.
    Statement 1 can be answered with <u>No, he don't.</u>; <u>No, he do
    not.</u>; <u>No, she don't.</u>; or <u>No, she do not.</u>

8. Since there is no convention for writing nonstandard pro-
    nunciation, there are three alternatives open to the

teacher and materials writer: the first is to use phonetic symbols; the second is to adapt some spelling
changes; and the third is to avoid writing nonstandard
pronunciations. In the following drills, the second
alternative has been adopted for the teacher's copy of
the drills; the third for teaching the drills to the
students.

9. In the drills shown in this paper, no verb is followed
    by a word beginning with a sibilant because it is im-
    possible to hear whether the verb ending is present:
    Robert plays center. and Robert play center. sound alike.
    In order to differentiate them, an unnatural extra syl-
    lable or pause would have to be inserted before center.

SOCIOLINGUISTIC IMPLICATIONS FOR

EDUCATIONAL SEQUENCING

by Walt Wolfram

Within the last several years the teaching of Standard English
to Black English speakers (i.e. the variety of English spoken
by lower socio-economic class Negroes) has been of growing concern to urban educators. Subsequently, materials for teaching
Standard English in an urban setting have been produced, and a
casual survey of these materials is sufficient to observe that
there are differing philosophical and methodological approaches
which characterize them. Furthermore, the features dealt with
in these lessons and the order in which the lessons are presented vary significantly.

Although the different philosophical and methodological
approaches underlying materials have now received some attention, one aspect of methodology for which there is no specific
discussion is the order in which Standard English features
should be presented. This failure may stem from the assumption that it is common knowledge which features of Standard
English should be given precedence in teaching Black English
speakers. However, if this were the case, one would expect
that all materials would conform to a similar pattern of sequencing, a situation which does not exist.

Another possible reason for the failure to deal with
pedagogical sequencing may stem from the assumption that the
ordering of lessons is irrelevant, that any order convenient
to the teacher is satisfactory. Several reasons can be suggested to challenge this assumption. First of all, both
objective and subjective evidence (see Wolfram 1969; Shuy,
Baratz and Wolfram 1969) suggest that not all features of

Black English have the same social connotations. There are
some features which immediately categorize the socio-economic
class of the speaker; others, however, may correlate with
ethnicity but have little or no social significance within
the black community. The fact that all features of Black
English do not have equal social connotations suggests that
some should be given precedence over others in the acquisition
of Standard English. Another reason for maintaining the relevancy of lesson sequencing is motivational. Students are much
more aware of the social consequences of Black English vis-à-
vis Standard English than they have been given credit for
(see Shuy, Baratz and Wolfram 1969), and the precedence of
minor rather than major differences between dialects may dis-
courage students at an early stage in their acquisition of
Standard English. A final reason is quite practical. The
realization that any course in Standard English will probably
not cover as much material as would be desirable means that
some features should be given priority over others in the
lesson material. One way of programming this priority into
the lesson material is through the sequencing of lessons.

Having suggested several reasons for the relevancy of
pedagogical sequencing, what criteria may be used in determining the relative order of the lessons? Several sociolinguistic factors can be suggested as a basis for determining the most relevant order of lessons.[1]

1. Social diagnosticity of linguistic variables

Since the purpose of teaching Standard English is to
assist students in adopting a dialect which is not socially
stigmatized, a primary consideration in the sequencing of
materials must be the way in which social groups are separated
from one another on the basis of linguistic features (i.e. the
social diagnosticity of linguistic items). As was stated
above, all linguistic features do not correlate with social
status in the same way. Some features set apart social groups
from one another much more discretely than others. Recently,

I have suggested (see Wolfram 1969) that it is useful to distinguish between gradient and sharp social stratification of
linguistic features. Gradient stratification refers to a
progressive increase in the frequency of occurrence of a
variant between social groups without a clearly defined difference between contiguous social groups. The incidence of
post-vocalic r in the black community is an example of gradient stratification. The following diagram illustrates the
differences in r absence for four social classes of Negroes
in Detroit, upper-middle (UMN), lower-middle (LMN), upper-
working (UWN), and lower-working (LWN) class Negroes.

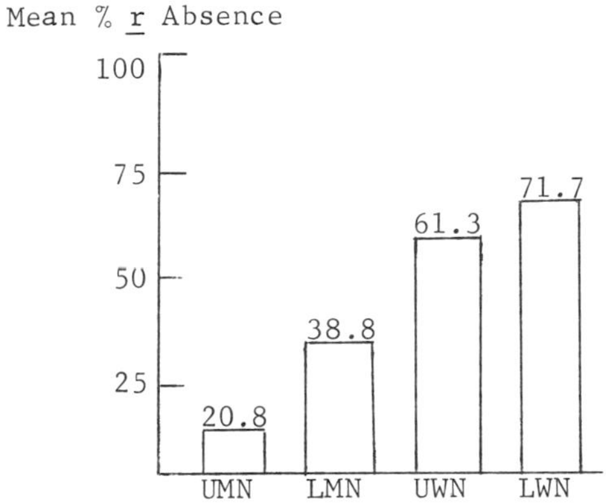

Mean % r Absence

Fig. 1. Post-vocalic r Absence: An Example of "Gradient"
         Stratification

One observes that there is a progressive increase in the
absence of post-vocalic r between the four social groups; none
of the groups are discretely differentiated on the basis of r.
But there are other variables which indicate a sharp demar-
cation between contiguous social classes (i.e. sharp stratification), such as the absence of third-person singular, present-
tense-s. Note the incidence of -s third person singular
absence in Fig. 2.

In contrast to the absence of post-vocalic r, we observe
that the middle class groups are sharply differentiated from
the working class groups by the incidence of -s. Contiguous
social groups (in this case, lower-middle and upper-working

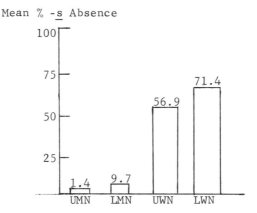

Fig. 2. Third Person Singular -s Absence: An Example
         of "Sharp" Stratification

classes) reveal significant differences in the incidence of
-s third-person singular. We conclude that linguistic features revealing sharp stratification are of greater social
significance than those showing gradient stratification.
From a social viewpoint, then, materials dealing with sharply
stratified linguistic features should precede those dealing
with gradiently stratified features.

　　Perhaps more important than the objective stratification
of linguistic features is the subjective reactions toward
these features.[2] Labov (1964: 102) has suggested that the
subjective evaluation of socially diagnostic linguistic features can be classified into three basic types:

　　　　indicators, which show social variation but usually
　　　　not stylistic variation, and have little effect upon
　　　　the listener's judgment of the social status of the
　　　　speakers

　　　　markers, which show both social and stylistic variation
　　　　and have consistent effects upon the conscious or un-
　　　　conscious judgment of the speaker's status by the
　　　　listener

　　　　stereotypes, which are the overt topics of social com-
　　　　ment in the speech community, and may or may not corres-
　　　　pond to actual linguistic behavior.

　　The different levels of subjective reaction to socially
diagnostic linguistic features have definite implications for

the ordering of materials. Materials should start with those
features which are on the most conscious level of awareness,
the stereotyped features. In terms of objective stratification, stereotyped features generally show sharp rather than
gradient stratification. Since, as Labov points out, there
are a number of stereotyped features which do not correspond
to actual sociolinguistic behavior, it must be warned that we
are referring to stereotyped features which relate to actual
speech. One must also warn that stereotyped features often
refer to single items, in which case they would not be given
precedence because they do not meet the criterion of rule
generality (cf. principle 2). One stereotyped feature of non-
standard speech (both Negro and white) is that of the so-called
"double negative" (but more accurately called "multiple negation") such as <u>He didn't do nothing</u>.

The relative social diagnosticity of a particular feature
may not only vary from linguistic variable to variable, but
within a given variable, based on independent linguistic con-
straints such as environment and structural type. Take, for
example, the absence of the final member of a consonant
cluster in word-final position (e.g. Black English /dɛs/ for
Standard English 'desk'). This type of pattern affects items
in which both members of the cluster are part of the same
lexical item (i.e. monomorphemic, as in Black English /gɛs/
for Standard English /gɛst/ 'guest') but also clusters which
result when the addition of the grammatical suffix -<u>ed</u> results in a cluster (i.e. bimorphemic clusters such as Black
English /gɛs/ for Standard English /gɛs-t/ 'guessed'). The
social significance of these two types are not equal, however. The former type, monomorphemic clusters, reveals a
gradient stratification whereas the latter, the bimorphemic
clusters, tend to reveal sharp stratification. In terms of
social importance, bimorphemic clusters would therefore take
precedence over monomorphemic. Likewise, in the analysis of

copula absence among Negro speakers, there are certain types
of constructions in which the absence of a copula is much
less socially significant than others. The absence of a
copula with the intentive future <u>gonna</u> (e.g. <u>They gonna go</u>
<u>now</u>) is commonly used by middle class Negro speakers although
they typically do not reveal copula absence in other types
of constructions such as predicative nominals, adjectives,
and locatives. It is plain that the presence of a copula
with <u>gonna</u> should follow the teaching of copula with other
types of constructions (e.g. predicate adjective such as <u>he</u>
<u>nice</u>) in preparing the lesson materials on copula.

2. <u>The generality of rules</u>

     Another important factor in determining the relative
order of materials is the generality of the rule(s) involved
in the realization of a particular Black English feature.
Some nonstandard forms affect only a small subset of words
or a single item whereas others involve general rules that
operate on the form of every sentence of a particular structural type. Labov and Cohen (1969: 1) note that:

> it is plain that the more general rules should be
> introduced first in a teaching program, no matter
> how prominent and striking the isolated items may be.

The more general the rule, the earlier it should be introduced in the materials. For example, the nonstandard use
of multiple negation affects all negative sentences with an
indefinite, including indefinite pronouns (e.g. <u>He didn't do</u>
<u>nothing</u>), determiners (e.g. <u>He didn't have no homework</u>), and
adverbs (e.g. <u>He hardly never does his homework</u>). On the
other hand, the Black English use of existential <u>it is</u> as a
correspondence of Standard English <u>there is</u> (e.g. Black English <u>It is a lot of trouble on that street</u>) only concerns one
item. Standard English lesson materials will probably deal
with both of these nonstandard features; however, based on
the generality of rules governing the nonstandard usage, it
should be obvious that multiple negation will appear in the

earliest stages of lessons but "existential it" in the later
lesson materials.

3. Phonological versus grammatical variables

In many current materials designed to teach Standard
English, it has sometimes been assumed that it makes little
difference whether one begins with phonological or grammatical
variables. Therefore, some materials focus on phonological
features before grammatical features while others reverse the
order. There is good reason to suggest that the teaching of
Standard English to Black English speakers should focus on
grammatical features before phonological features. In the
first place, the social significance of phonological and
grammatical features tend to differ. In my description of
four phonological and four grammatical variables, it was
pointed out that there is an important difference between the
social diagnosticity of phonological and grammatical variables
(Wolfram 1969). Grammatical features tend to show sharp
stratification whereas phonological variables tend to reveal
gradient stratification.[3] Three of the four phonological
variables investigated reveal gradient stratification, but
all four variables which were treated as grammatical indicate
sharp stratification.[4] As a general principle then, it is
safest to begin with grammatical rather than phonological
features.

Another factor favoring the introduction of grammatical
features first is the type of differences observed between
social groups. The social distribution of grammatical features show that there are qualitative differences between
groups; that is, middle class groups often indicate complete
absence of certain grammatical variants (such as multiple
negation, suffixal -s absence, 'distributive be', etc.) which
are present in working class speech. But phonological features most often reveal quantitative differences between
social groups. Thus, d for potential ð in word-initial

position (in such words as then, that, those), the lack of
constriction for post-vocalic r (in words like car, beard,
mother), the absence of the final member of a consonant
cluster (in words like desk, ground, cold), monophthongization of potential upgliding diphthongs (in words like time,
ground, boil), and syllable final t for d (in words like
good, bad, stupid) all reveal quantitative differences between social groups. Qualitative differences tend to be more
socially obtrusive than quantitative differences and therefore should be taught first. In some cases phonological and
grammatical patterns intersect with one another to account
for certain stigmatized features. We have already seen how
this can happen with word-final consonant clusters. To take
an example of a somewhat different type, consider the Black
English use of invariant be in a sentence such as he be home.
There is evidence to consider that this construction is derived from three different sources, two of which are phonological and one grammatical (see Fasold 1969; Wolfram 1969).
Invariant be may be derived from an underlying will be in a
sentence such as He be in pretty soon; in a sentence such as
If he had a walkie talkie, he be happy it is derived from
would be; but in a sentence such as He be busy all the time,
it is the realization of a grammatical category unique to the
Black English speaker, "distributive be". Although one may
initially assume that all three uses of be are equally stigmatized, there is good reason to suggest that this is not the
case. In the first place, the negative formations of these
three constructions in Black English are He won't be in in a
few minutes, If he had a walkie talkie he wouldn't be happy,
and He don't be busy all the time respectively. Only the
last example is socially obtrusive to the middle class speaker.

    A second reason for suggesting that "distributive be" is
more socially stigmatized than the other two uses is that
Standard English speakers sometimes produce a contracted form

of will be ('ll) and would be ('d) which is phonetically not
very different from the first two uses of be. But no Standard
English speaker would ever use be in its distributive sense.
We thus see that where the intersection of phonological and
grammatical patterns takes place, grammatical differences
between Standard English and Black English should be given
precedence.

4. Regional versus general social significance

    Many large Northern urban areas have been drastically
restructured within the last 50 years because of the in-
migration of Southern Negroes. Due to the extent of the
intersectional migration and the segregation patterns of
such in-migrants in the North, the speech patterns of many
Negroes living in the North have not been adapted to a Northern dialect of English. In a Northern locale, some features
which are acceptable Southern speech patterns have been transformed into class and ethnic patterns. Thus, in a city such
as Detroit, "r-lessness", the neutralization of the ɪ/ɛ contrast before nasals, and monophthongization[5] of potential
upgliding diphthongs have taken on a social significance even
though they are acceptable patterns used by the middle class
in certain parts of the South. On the other hand, there are
a number of factors which have social significance regardless
of the regional locale in which they are found. Thus, the
absence of third person singular, present-tense -s, the use
of invariant be, and multiple negation are socially diagnostic
in all regions of the United States.

    Several reasons can be suggested why features having
general social significance should be dealt with before those
whose social significance is regionally restricted (e.g. just
in a Northern city). First, those features which reveal
general social significance tend to be more socially diagnostic than those showing only regional significance. In
terms of our distinction between sharp and gradient stratification, one observes that in Northern cities, acceptable

Southern features reveal gradient rather than sharp stratification among the Negro population. But general nonstandard
features often show sharp stratification. We thus see that
our distinction between features showing regional and general
social significance correlates in an important way with relative social diagnosticity of items.

Second, in terms of the widest possible audience of students for lesson materials, general features should be given
priority over regional features. Recent investigations of
Black English in a number of big cities in the United States
indicate that there is a "common core" of Black English
characteristic of lower socio-economic Negroes in different
regions. This observation means that lesson materials may be
produced which can be used in more than one region. However,
to develop materials for the broadest possible use, the general socially diagnostic features should be given precedence
over the regionally significant items. By placing these
regionally significant features in later stages of lessons
(if they are to be included at all) their relative importance
can be appropriately diminished (i.e. they can easily be
excluded where not applicable or, in terms of time limita-
tions, where lessons can most conveniently be eliminated or
condensed). Although one might think that this principle is
obvious to those responsible for developing lessons, many
current materials are surprisingly negligent in this regard.
Some teachers have taken far too much interest in relatively
minor features such as the monophthongization of upgliding
diphthongs (e.g. /tahm/ 'time', /bɔh/ 'boy') and the neutralization of the ɪ/ɛ contrast before nasals (e.g. /pɪn/ 'pin'
or 'pen'), although these are quite acceptable patterns used
by middle class Southerners. In justification of such
interest, some teachers explain that if such differences are
not taught, the students will be unable to discriminate between such words as pin and pen. While this may certainly be
the case (apart from contextual disambiguation), this common

type of "interdialectal homophony" (i.e. distinguishable words
in one dialect are indistinguishable in another dialect) is no
need for concern. It is a common phenomenon of dialects which
have kept dialectologists busy and non-linguists amused for
some time now. The same teachers who may attempt to spend
inordinate amounts of time drilling students to contrast pin
and pen may make no distinction between cot and caught in
their own speech without ever having noticed it. Although it
may sound unnecessarily judgmental, the preoccupation with
such items as pin and pen, while well-intentioned, may ultimately be traced to dialectal ethnocentrism.

5. The relative frequency of items

      A final factor in the determination of lesson sequencing
is the relative frequency with which an item or pattern potentially occurs. Some nonstandard patterns occur only infrequently during the course of a normal discourse. Even though
some of these features may indicate sharp stratification, the
infrequency of their occurrence makes them less essential than
others in preparing lesson materials. For example, a comparison of the potential incidence of third-person singular
present-tense -s with the posessive marker -s for 48 Detroit
informants reveals that the former structural pattern is over
four times as numerous as the latter (see Wolfram 1969). It
is therefore understandable why many people are more con-
sciously aware of the absence of -s on third person forms
than they are of the absence of -s on possessives.

      Another example of a relatively infrequent occurring
feature is the Black English use of been as an auxiliary in
active sentence such as The boy been ate the pie. Although
this use of been clearly correlates to social class in the
Negro community, the rarity of this type of construction in
natural discourse suggests that the "non-use" of this type
of form should only be taught after many other features which
occur much more frequently.

6. The intersection of sociolinguistic principles in determining the sequencing of materials

When determining the order of lessons, each Black English feature must be considered in terms of the total con-
figuration of sociolinguistic principles. The fact that a
particular item reveals sharp stratification is, in itself,
not adequate for including it in the preliminary stages of
the lessons. Nor is the distinction of frequent versus infrequent patterns sufficient reason for determining order by
itself. Only when the intersection of the various principles
is considered can an adequate justification for sequencing be
established. The determination of order may be viewed in
terms of a sociolinguistic matrix. In Fig. 3, a number of
features cited as examples in the above discussion are evaluated in terms of such a matrix. For the most part, the
evaluation is based on a binary opposition (e.g. either an
item is considered frequent [+] or infrequent [-]). Where
binary judgments cannot be made (e.g. the intersection of
phonology and grammar or different levels of social significance based on subcategories of a variable) this is indicated by [±].

The way the matrix is set up, the more [+] evaluations
a particular feature has, the earlier it should be introduced
in the lesson material. This means that items given a [+]
rating for all of the sociolinguistic principles should be
introduced at the earliest stage, those with more [+] than
[-] ratings at the next stage, and those with more [-] than
[+] ratings at a still later stage. Such features as -s
third person singular, multiple negation, and invariant be
(particularly its grammatical source) should be treated in
the earliest lessons. A next stage should deal with such
features as word-medial and final θ and consonant clusters,
whereas features such as ɪ/ɛ contrast before nasals, syllable
final d, and post-vocalic r should clearly be treated in the
later lessons.

Black English Feature	sharp stratification [+] / gradient stratification [-]	general rule [+] / non-general rule [-]	grammatical feature [+] / phonological feature [-]	general significance [+] / regional significance [-]	frequent occurrence [+] / infrequent occurrence [-]
-s third person singular (e.g. he go)	+	+	+	+	+
multiple negation (e.g. didn't do nothing)	+	+	+	+	+
-s possessive (e.g. man hat)	+	+	+	+	-
invariant be (e.g. he be home)	+	+	±	+	+
copula absence (e.g. he nice)	+	+	-	+	+
been auxiliary in active sentence (e.g. he been ate the food)	+	-	+	+	-
existential it (e.g. It is a whole lot of people)	+	-	+	+	+
word-medial and final ð and θ (e.g. /tuf/ 'tooth')	+	+	-	+	+
word-final consonant clusters (e.g. /gɛs/ 'guest' and 'guessed')	±	+	-	+	+
word-initial ð (e.g. /dɛn/ 'then')	-	+	-	+	+
monophthongization (e.g. /tahm/ 'time')	-	+	-	-	+
post-vocalic r and l (e.g. /cah/ 'car')	-	+	-	-	+
syllable-final d (e.g. /bɛht/ 'bad')	-	+	-	-	+
ı/ε before nasals (e.g. /pɪn/ 'pin' or 'pen')	-	-	-	-	-

Fig. 3. Matrix of Cruciality

I have attempted to show how sociolinguistic considera-
tions have important implications for teaching Standard English to Black English speakers. The application of these
five principles can only increase the sociolinguistic relevancy of Standard English programs and improve their efficiency.

NOTES

1. The limitation of this discussion to sociolinguistic fac-
    tors is not meant to imply that other factors may not
    affect the ordering of materials. For example, the
    pedogogical lessons on constructions introduced earlier
    may affect the order of items to a certain extent. Since
    the focus of this paper is the sociolinguistic factors,
    other factors will not be considered here.

2. Shuy, Baratz and Wolfram (1969) show that lower socio-
    economic class speakers who use stigmatized variants
    often have the same low opinion of these forms as do
    middle class speakers who do not use them. Therefore
    the label "stigmatized" refers to a working class as well
    as a middle class evaluation of such forms.

3. McDavid (1965:15) notes that "the surest social markers
    in American English are grammatical forms, and any teach-
    ing program should aim, first of all, at developing a
    habitual command of the grammar of Standard English".

4. This does not mean that ALL socially diagnostic gram-
    matical features reveal sharp stratification or that ALL
    phonological features show gradient stratification since
    research does not show this to be the case. For example,
    the Black English correspondence of Standard English θ
    and δ in certain positions, which is f and v respectively,
    shows sharp stratification. On the other hand, the Black
    English use of pronominal apposition (e.g. The man, he
    did it) is a grammatical feature which reveals gradient
    stratification.

5. Monophthongization is technically not quite correct for
    the pronunciation of 'time' as [taɔm] instead of [taym].
    The distinction actually is found in the direction of the
    glide; in the former case there is a central glide and in
    the latter a high front glide. Fo convenience in this
    paper, the central gliding variant will be referred to as
    monophthongization.

BIBLIOGRAPHY

Fasold, Ralph W.   1969.   "Tense and the Form be in Black
English".   Language 45:763-776.

Labov, William and Paul Cohen.   1964.   "Stages in the Acquisition of Standard English", Social Dialects and Language Learning, ed. by Roger W. Shuy.   Champaign, National
Council of Teachers of English.

McDavid, Raven I.   1966.   "Sense and Nonsense about American
Dialects", Publications of the Modern Language Association
of America, 81:7-17.

Shuy, Roger, Joan C. Baratz and Walter A. Wolfram.   1969.
Sociolinguistic Factors in Speech Identification.   Final
Report, Research Project No. MH 15048-01, National Insti-
tute of Mental Health.

Wolfram, Walter A.   1969.   A Sociolinguistic Description of
Detroit Negro Speech.   Washington, D.C., Center for Applied
Linguistics.

TEACHER TRAINING AND URBAN LANGUAGE PROBLEMS[1]

by Roger W. Shuy

Back in the days when the universe was orderly, when subject
matter was a fixed commodity and methodology was a science,
we knew exactly how to train teachers to meet the daily needs
of their students. In that by-gone time there was a rather
clear separation of the disciplines and, although we talked
a great deal about suiting the teaching strategy to the individual needs of each student, nobody really paid any attention to this dictum and it can be strongly suspected that
nobody really believed it anyway. We gave prospective teachers a strong dose of educational history, theory and method
along with the appropriate courses in "special methods of."
There was a good bit of talk about slow learners but they
were quickly siphoned off to vocational education tracks and
those who were discipline problems were encouraged, in one
way or another to "seek employment as soon as possible to
insure economic adjustment."

But now the times have caught up with us. We have painted
ourselves into the corner of compulsory attendance in the
schools. We have developed a generation of people who are
rightfully demanding relevance. All these years of talking
about "meeting the child where he is" have come back to us
with interest, for it has become clear that research is finally catching up with precept and, quite simply, it is time to
practice what we preach. In this essay I will attempt to point
out a path toward preparing teachers to do this practicing.
First I will assess the current situation, then prescribe a
remedy.

What Do Teachers Know About Language?

Relatively little research has been done on what the teacher knows, feels or thinks about the language of disadvantaged pupils. Considerable data have been gathered on how a teacher is trained, on whether or not he feels adequately trained, and on what he actually does in the process of teaching. But sophisticated assessments of what teachers really know about the language used by children and how they feel about it are scarce. We know from The National Interest and the Teaching of English that the linguistic preparation of prospective English teachers is woefully inadequate. It should not be surprising, then, that teachers find it difficult to describe accurately the language problems of their disadvantaged students. As an adjunct to recent research on Detroit speech, thirty urban teachers were randomly selected and asked to identify the language problems of their students who were designated, in one way or another, as disadvantaged.[2]

Vocabulary

Eighty percent of the teachers observed that their students have a limited vocabulary and many teachers offered a reason for this handicap:

> "In the program, the children come with a very meager vocabulary, I would say. I think it's because of the background of the home and the lack of books at home, the lack of communication with the family, especially, if there are only one or two children in the family. Perhaps if there are more children in the family communication might be a bit better. They might have a few more words in their vocabulary".

> "In the inner-city, the child's vocabulary is very limited. His experiences are very limited".

These comments are typical in that the home situation is blamed for the limited vocabulary. Neither teacher gave any indication that the home environment might produce a different vocabulary. On the contrary, both felt that lack of school vocabulary was equivalent to a lack of overall vocabulary.

This widely held but erroneous concept (that "disadvantaged" children have limited vocabularies) appears to stem
from fairly recent research reports on the language of the
disadvantaged child. Yet, nothing in the current research
of sociolinguists supports this idea. Several different
reasons can be given for the rise of the notion that children
in disadvantaged homes have limited vocabularies. It may be
that the investigators proved to be such a cultural barrier
to the informants that they were too frightened and awed to
talk freely, or that the investigators simply asked the wrong
questions or that the interviewee's life-style simply requires a different lexicon.

The interviewed teachers' misconceptions about the size
of a disadvantaged child's vocabulary may be illustrated as
follows:

> "Some had a vocabulary of about a hundred and some words,
> I'd say; no more than that. They got along fine with
> what they knew. They didn't have any trouble expressing
> themselves. They knew the important words for them to
> get along okay. Some could talk your foot off. I mean,
> they just knew everything. The quieter ones were the
> ones who didn't have a large vocabulary".

The absurdity of assuming that a child has only a hundred
words or so is one of the curious stereotypes of the teaching
profession. What is more distressing than this hyperbole,
however, is the condescending tone ("they got along fine with
what they knew") and the assumption that quiet children are
quiet because they have no vocabulary.

Grammar

The responses of these teachers to the grammar problems
of their disadvantaged students is equally naive. One third
of the teachers characterized the child's greatest problem
as his failure to speak in sentences and/or complete thoughts:

> "I can't get them to make a sentence. Even if I have
> them repeat after me exactly, they don't do it. They
> repeat in sentences they are familiar with. They're
> not really sentences but fragments of sentences that
> are familiar to them, and they understand them. They
> don't realize that they aren't making a complete thought".

"Where we would use a sentence to convey a thought,
they are in the habit of maybe using a phrase or just
a few words to try to convey the same thought which I
would presume would affect their communication to a
great extent".

Although 30% of the teachers described their students'
grammar as poor and/or limited, one might seriously question
some teachers' understanding of what grammar means. They
offered the following comments on the grammar of their students:

"The biggest problem that I've had so far is 'I'm
gonna'".

"Because there is no real honest communication between
parent and child, the child isn't taught to listen.
He doesn't hear; he doesn't enunciate, you see".

"These children cut words off: 'could' would be 'ould',
such as in 'Ould you like to do this?' Too, their
'l's' were often missing".

Even when their responses reflected a clearer distinction between phonology and grammar, the description was often
not accurate enough to be diagnostically useful.

"Their grammar problems are many because they use sub-
stitutions, this for that".

"They use too many personal pronouns".

As for current pedagogical technique, there is little to
choose from if the teachers' responses are considered as a
guide:

"I introduce the verb to children as an action word
showing them what they're doing and the noun as the
name of the person or place. That helps them write and
speak in a complete sentence".

"When I say, 'Where can I get a pencil?', they will
answer, 'Here it goes'. It is hard for them to say
'Here it is', but if I talk enough about it, they may
change".

Pronunciation

The teachers generally had more to say about pronunciation than vocabulary or grammar. Again there were over-
generalizations such as:

"I have one child who mispronounces almost every word,
but they say he does not have a speech problem".

"Many times they mispronounce because they do not know
the sounds".

"They do have trouble with pronunciation for they fail
to use their teeth and tongue and their lips. This is
necessary for getting the correct sound".

"Their trouble was the use of dialect for they said hal
for how. It was southern dialect among some of the
children which caused them to use the wrong words".

"Pronunciation is poor. Things like, 'I wanna go', or
'punkin' for 'pumpkin' and things like that. Their
dialect is just hard to understand for most teachers.
We were born and raised in the Midwest, for the most
part".

It is indeed difficult to imagine anyone using language who
fails to use his teeth and tongue and lips. The supposed substitution of hal for how indicates an awareness of the l
problem in non-standard English but a confusion about the
nature of the problem (the l is not inserted, it is deleted).
The parochialism of the last quotation is unsound since it
is an easy matter to cite pronunciations of wanna for want to
in the speech of any prestigous American.

As for specific kinds of pronunciation problems, the
teachers agreed rather clearly that disadvantaged children
delete word final consonant sounds:

"They leave off last sounds, leave off beginning sounds
some times. But then I have that trouble now even with
the other children. I keep saying to them to put in all
the letters for that's why they're there".

"Some of the children had problems with their consonants,
particularly at the ends of words".

"They leave off the endings of words; instead of 'going'
it's 'goin'. (Also the d's and t's give them trouble.)
Even at the beginning of words you often cannot hear the
beginning letter".

"I think that they're in the habit of not saying the
things as clearly as we do and they say a word as 'looking' by leaving the g off".

The teachers' confusion of sounds and orthography is perhaps
to be expected (for it seems widespread in the country) but
it may be confusing to a first grade child to be told to add
a g when the ng combination stands for a single sound.

On the other hand, these teachers came a bit closer to
some of the significant problems of disadvantaged pronunciation than they did for vocabulary or grammar. 17% cited
the /ŋ → n/ substitution, for example. In general, however,
the analyses were too vague to be diagnostically useful.
A major point, is that there is a pattern in inner-city
speech -- just as there is pattern in every kind of speech.
The teacher neither described the problem accurately nor
understood its pattern.

One of the most important aspects of problems of language
development among disadvantaged children, therefore, centers
on imprecise descriptions of the problem, large scale ignorance of how to make such a description and extant folklore
which passes as knowledge about a vastly neglected and under-
privileged group of human beings. Having said this, it is
no difficult matter to say that the current linguistic
sophistication of teachers is rather limited.

What Do Teachers Need To Know About Language?

Extant attempts to prepare teachers adequately for the
classroom of the disadvantaged student are disappointingly
weak. Few undergraduate courses are offered in subjects even
remotely related to the linguistic aspects of the problem.
Even occasional college courses such as The Nature of Language, Introductory Linguistics, Modern Grammar, American
English, etc. are seldom offered and, if offered, seldom required of teachers and, if required of teachers, seldom
geared to minority language problems. Thus the anomaly
exists. Although one of the most urgent situations in our
schools focuses on the language problems of blacks and other
minority groups, there is virtually no preparation for dealing with such problems in the college curricula.[3]

Part of the reason why such courses have been slow to develop is found in the suddenness and recentness of our discovery of the problem. Although English teachers have long wrestled with the problem of making acceptable speakers of English out of non-standard speakers, it is only with the recent emphasis on urban problems, black awareness and a new kind of social responsibility that we have given serious consideration to the specific problems of minority groups, the black, urban poor in particular. Then, as is often the case in education, the need for teaching materials preceded any strongly felt need for theoretical bases or empirical research upon which such materials could be based. As absurd as it may seem to produce classroom materials before establishing a theoretical base for their development, that is exactly what has happened in this field today. To complicate matters even more, some sensitive teachers, realizing that their training has not been adequate for their needs, are now asking for that training, preferably in condensed and intensive packages. As healthy as this situation may appear to be, it has only triggered still another problem -- that of finding adequately trained professionals who can provide this training. Ideally what is needed at the moment is more training of professional basic researchers in the field, more application of this basic research to pedagogy and more programs for training teacher-intermediaries to use these materials and techniques in the classrooms. Although the focus of this essay is on the latter, it is difficult to separate the training of teachers from basic research, for good teacher training cannot be separated from an understanding of the motives and results of the basic researchers.

Without apology, then, let me suggest that teachers need to know about the current research in urban language problems. It would be helpful if they knew why the research is being done, something about how it is carried out, what is known

at the moment and, every bit as important, what is not known.
Further, teachers need to assess their own language in relation to that of their pupils. They need to understand language variation -- the reasons underlying it and the attitudes
of various subgroups toward it. Teachers should be trained to
listen to the language of their students. They should learn
how systematic various dialects can be and they should develop
a sensitivity to the editing processes that take place as one
person listens to another. The teacher should learn enough
about foreign language methodology to be able to handle material of the sort discussed by Irwin Feigenbaum (pp. 87-104) and
they should learn enough about sociolinguistics to be able to
understand and make use of suggestions of the sort made by
William Stewart (pp. 1-19), Ralph Fasold and Walt Wolfram
(pp. 41-86), and Walt Wolfram (pp. 105-119).

It should be clear from the outset, however, that the
suggestions which follow are not intended to constitute a
mere appendage to the already existing teacher training program. Elsewhere I have expressed the strong feeling that the
traditional language arts teacher preparation program gives
far too much attention to matters of administration, teaching
techniques, and methods of evaluation at the expense of the
study of language, the real content of their teaching.[4] (A
recent national conference on educating the disadvantaged
devoted less than 5% of its attention during the two days of
meetings to the content of such education. Practically all
of the papers and discussion centered on funding such programs, administrating them and evaluating them.)

Although it seems ludicrous to have to say so, the
preparation of language arts teachers must be overhauled to
put language at the center of the program, accompanied wherever possible by courses in administration, techniques and
evaluation. By far the most important tool for survival,
for communicating and for obtaining knowledge and skills is

language. For children, this is an indisputable fact. It is
as true for middle class children as for disadvantaged socio-
economic groups. But if the circumstances under which poor
children acquire this tool militate in some way against their
acquiring middle class language patterns, some kind of special
attention must be given them. This special attention requires
of the teacher:

1. An ability to recognize and react adequately to con-
    trastive language patterns.

2. An ability to do something about them when appropriate.

3. An ability to keep from doing something about them
    when appropriate.

Earlier we observed that there is no evidence to date which
indicates that we are training teachers adequately to handle
#1. There is relatively little in the way of materials geared
to accommodate #2. There is practically no understanding of
#3 among teachers or, for that matter, among textbook writers.

In short, what teachers need to know in order to fulfill
their educational obligations to the ghetto child (or, in
fact, to any child) is how to deal with the child's language,
how to listen and respond to it, how to diagnose what is
needed, how to best teach alternate linguistic systems and
how to treat it as a positive and healthy entity. What follows will include a brief and speculative effort to formalize
these requirements in terms of the traditional course structure of our educational system.

How Should They Be Taught?

Experience during the past two or three years has taught
us that there is no magic package which is guaranteed to produce adequately trained teachers in short periods of time.
A summer workshop or institute may be helpful if it is specific to a well defined aspect of the necessary training but
it is doubtful that such a program can come close to covering
the required material or that it will provide maturation time

to accommodate the new thought-set which is demanded. Several
pre-service college courses may contribute significantly to
the proper linguistic perspective. I will first propose what
these college courses might contain, then consider ways of
covering this same material in in-service training programs.

Suggested College Courses

     1. The Nature of Language. It will be quite useful for
later discussion of language variation and change, foreign
language learning techniques, grammatical and phonological
features, etc. if the basic linguistic tools are covered in
an introductory course. In this course, special attention
will be placed on language attitudes. Various tests will be
administered at the beginning of the course as a measure of
entry attitudes and knowledge and as a point for later discussion. These tests could be at several levels of abstraction. One, for example, might have only written stimuli of
the following sort:

        a. Language Stereotype Index

T F 1. Language change will ultimately cause degreda-
         tion in the language.

T F 2. A speaker should avoid using dialect at all times.

T F 3. There is no evidence to support the claim that
         there is a relationship between climatic heat and
         slowness of speech.

T F 4. Poor black children speak a version of English
         which has system and regularity.

T F 5. To improve one's social acceptability to a middle
         class society, working class people should focus
         primarily on vocabulary development.

    One difficulty with abstract test questions such as the
ones illustrated above is that it is difficult to determine
exactly how much of the teacher's attitude is attributable to
actual language attitude and how much stems from a kind of
stereotyped inheritance. That is, is the teacher's attitude
a real one or one that he feels should be given under these

circumstances. A teacher, for example, may not personally
care about or believe in teaching children on an individual
basis but when asked about useful techniques of teaching she
may well utter the term, "individualized instruction." It
is because of this tendency that I refer to the above type
of test as a language stereotype index.

Another type of attitude measurement is considerably
less abstract. The stimulus, in this case, is a tape recording of people talking. Center for Applied Linguistics researchers have used one of the audio-tapes originally prepared for the Psycholinguistic Attitude Study as an introduction to discussions about social dialect variation. Following is a typescript of one segment of this tape:

b. Tape Stimulus Index

I just look at it some time and then somtime I be busy.
I just half look at it. I never hardly look at one all
the way through. I never found one that was too much
of a favorite. We used to go (to) the theater alot you
know. Well it all blends in the same thing like that.
And a guy just look at it so often well you don't care
too much about it.

The listener is asked to respond to this tape recording
by answering the following (or other similar) questions:

1. What is the race of this speaker?

   Negro ( )   White ( )

2. What is the educational/occupational level of this
   speaker?

   ( ) a. College graduate usually with graduate
            training. Dentist, mechanical engineer,
            personnel manager.

   ( ) b. High School graduate, probably some college
            or technical school. Printer, post office
            clerk, small business owner or manager.

   ( ) c. Some high school, or high school graduate.
            Bus driver, carpenter, telephone lineman.

   ( ) d. Not beyond 8th grade. Dishwasher, night
            watchman, construction laborer.

3. Rate the speech sample on each of the following
    scales:

correct ___: ___: ___: ___: ___: ___: ___: incorrect

awkward ___: ___: ___: ___: ___: ___: ___: graceful

relaxed ___: ___: ___: ___: ___: ___: ___: tense

formal ___: ___: ___: ___: ___: ___: ___: informal

clear   ___: ___: ___: ___: ___: ___: ___: thick

As it turns out, this particular subject is Negro and fits
category 2c. Answers to Question 3, which is more evaluative,
will probably relate to the answers previously given to 1 and
2. An interesting variation of this procedure would be to
ask only one question at a time, playing the same tape three
times (mixed between other passages). This procedure might
help reduce the potential influence of one answer or another.
But, of course, the test is not to determine how accurate the
listeners can be, as much as to serve as a take-off point for
a following discussion. Why did the listener think the speaker
was Negro? What clues led him to suspect that he was 2c?
Why does he consider him relaxed? The very doing of this
exercise clearly illustrates the future teachers' need to be
able to develop a vocabulary for talking about language differences with accuracy and precision. It can alert the teachers to their critical need to hear phonological differences
which have social consequences. It forces them to abandon
their reliance on stereotypes about language and to listen on
their own. Listening to the same tape at a later time will
also show them something about how we severely edit what we
listen to and, ultimately, hear what we want to hear.

Still another type of language attitude test focuses not
on stereotyped ideas about language or tape recorded stimuli
but on language concepts. Again the Psycholinguistic Attitude
Study provides a clue to the sort of question which might be

asked. In this study, the following language concepts were presented: Detroit Speech, White Southern Speech, British Speech, Negro Speech and Standard Speech. These were presented, on paper, in the following manner:

1. Detroit Speech

slow	__: __: __: __: __: __: __:	fast
simple	__: __: __: __: __: __: __:	complex
valuable	__: __: __: __: __: __: __:	worthless
bad	__: __: __: __: __: __: __:	good
thick	__: __: __: __: __: __: __:	clear
sloppy	__: __: __: __: __: __: __:	careful
smooth	__: __: __: __: __: __: __:	rough
negative	__: __: __: __: __: __: __:	positive
easy	__: __: __: __: __: __: __:	difficult
sharp	__: __: __: __: __: __: __:	dull
dumb	__: __: __: __: __: __: __:	smart
strong	__: __: __: __: __: __: __:	weak

Many other situations might be studied including, School Speech, Playground Talk, Political Addresses, etc. Likewise, other polar adjectives might be used, particularly those which have evaluative functions.

Some language attitude studies, then, would provide a starting point for the introductory course in the nature of language. From these, stress should be placed on phonetics (in order to learn how to recognize and produce phonetic differences) and on the study of grammar (with a number of problems to be solved). The systematic nature of language should be emphasized throughout.

2. Language Variation. Once certain tools for discussing language have been established, it is possible to approach language variation more adequately. Since geographical variation is generally recognized by most people, it seems reasonable to use regional dialects as a beginning point. There are several books, records and tapes available for illustra-

tive purposes. Emphasis should be placed on the systematic
nature of geographical differences, whether grammatical,
phonological or lexical. A certain amount of data gathering
in all three categories is desirable, both for practice in
the subject matter mastered in The Nature of Language and
practice in getting used to discovering and describing language patterns systematically.

Once geographical variation is fairly well studied, the
major portion of the course should focus on social dialects.
Attention should be given to problems of the relationship of
attitudes to labeling (Black English, ghetto speech, disadvantaged language, non-standard Negro English, Negro dialect, Texmex, etc.) but the major focus should reflect the
recent work of sociolinguists. The course should contain
units on the historical origins of current non-standard grammatical and phonological features (including correlations with
social stratification), frequency of occurrence and social
diagnosticity. Early attention should be given the concepts
of linguistic variation, the linguistic continuum and matters
of style shifting. The concept of language interference must
be emphasized particularly in relation to interference caused
by the system of various non-standards on the system of standard. This concept may be most easily presented by observing
the influence of the Spanish system on the production of English by people of Spanish speaking ancestry. Since many of
these people constitute a large portion of the disadvantaged
in our country anyway, the example is doubly useful. Once
the notion of linguistic interference is introduced across
different language systems, it may be easier to teach the
notion of linguistic interference across two dialects.

3. Fieldwork in the Language of Children. This course
should be primarily an experience in gathering language data
and analysis of certain linguistic features. Near the beginning of the course students carefully review the details

of field techniques, especially matters relating to selection
of subject, recording techniques, and methods of elicitation
(see Dan Slobin, ed., A Field Manual for Cross-Cultural Study
of the Acquisition of Communicative Competence, Berkeley,
U. of California, 1967 and R. Shuy, W. Wolfram and W. Riley,
Field Techniques in an Urban Language Study, Washington, CAL,
1968). Special attention should be given to different techniques of language data elicitation such as sentence imitation,
word games, narratives, citation forms, oral reading, dialog
and communicative routines for the linguistic responses may
well relate to the elicitation mode.

It is difficult to determine exactly how such a course
should be conducted but one thing is of utmost importance:
the students should get deeply involved in recording and
analyzing the language of at least one child-subject. One
technique which I have found useful toward this end is to
require each student to get at least an hour of tape recorded,
interview style data from one disadvantaged child in a nearby
community. It makes little difference what the child talks
about as long as there is a great deal of his speech and as
little of that of the interviewer as possible. Subjects for
discussion will vary somewhat but most people can describe
television programs or movies and almost everyone can tell
you how to play a game of some sort. The value of such an
exercise may be observed from a report of one of my students
in a recent experienced teacher class called Problems in Urban
Language:

> I talked to Reynaldo for 40 minutes and he thought I
> was the dumbest white woman he had ever seen. I was
> trying to remember all that I had been told about
> interviewing and drawing out an informant. As you
> will see, I had to act ignorant about basketball,
> football, and even the name of our nation's capital!
> You will be interested to know that during the inter-
> view I didn't hear any errors in his speech. I was
> terribly disappointed. Later, as I listened to it for
> the third time I thought I detected a few; but it
> wasn't until I wrote down every single word that I
> realized the many interesting features in his speech.

This teacher's remarks about the outwardly simple task of listening analytically to the speech of a child are typical of most teachers who have been forced to do this sort of thing. At first, they can't imagine why they were subjected to this assignment. They are even more dismayed when they are required to typescript the entire tape recording, using standard orthography (no attempt at reflecting pronunciation).[5] This process is time consuming and laborious but it serves several important purposes:

1. It forces the listener to listen carefully to the tape recording. During the early analysis stages of the Detroit Dialect Study in 1966, several Detroit teachers were temporarily employed doing this sort of typescripting. After three or four days of solid listening one of them remarked to me that although she had been teaching in a Head Start school for several years, she had never really listened to these children before. Just the task of listening and typescripting, then, served a useful function.

2. It provides a reference point for further listening and for future grammatical and phonological analysis. Anyone who has worked with long tape-recordings knows the amount of time it takes just to find the place he is looking for. If there is a typescript to accompany the tape, one can mark in advance the potential spots where the phonological feature under consideration is likely to occur. In the case of grammatical features, the typescript may itself be adequate for analytical procedures.

When the field interview and typescripting are completed, students should be required to select one or more interesting grammatical and phonological features for thorough analysis, including a search of the available literature and a description which calls upon and uses what they have learned about language analysis to this time.

4. <u>Teaching Standard English to the Disadvantaged Child</u>.
As in the preceding courses, this course should be problem
oriented. Two problems of great magnitude might occupy the
attention of the class near the beginning of the course.
Considerable ink has been spilled in an as yet unsuccessful
attempt to define the disadvantaged. However trite this may
seem, it is important that students realize the quandry we
are in whenever we start to discuss the topic. The second
problem may come as a surprise to the students. Standard
English is equally difficult to define. An early project,
then, might be to require all students to try to define standard English in a page or less of text. Chances are that they
will find their own papers unsatisfactory. Some will refer
to dictionaries, some will argue from sociological or political grounds, some will opt for the mass media as the norm
and some will say that it is what is taught in the schools.
Any answer should bring forth a challenge from other students
in the class.

There is a small but interesting body of literature on
the nature of "standard language" which has been written in
recent years by linguists (see, for example, Punya Sloka Ray,
"Language Standardization" in Frank A. Rice, ed., <u>Study of the
Role of Second Languages</u>, Washington, CAL, 1962; William Labov,
"Stages in the Acquisition of Standard English" in Roger Shuy,
ed., <u>Social Dialects and Language Learning</u>, Champaign, NCTE,
1965, and Otto Jesperson, <u>Mankind, Nation and Individual</u>,
Bloomington, Indiana U. Press, 1946).

After this introduction, the bulk of the course will be
taken up by the study of biloquialism. The other articles in
this publication are of great concern for the study of this
subject. Students should be introduced to foreign language
teaching techniques and there should be discussion of how
these techniques apply to learning standard English. Students
should then be guided in an examination of extant oral language

materials for non-standard speakers (Lin 1964, Golden 1965, Hurst 1965, Feigenbaum 1970) and they should review the literature on the relationship of second dialect acquisition in the appropriate journals.

A worthwhile project in such a course would be the construction of teaching materials which deal with features the students analyzed in their earlier fieldwork experiences. It should be clear, however, that the students are not expected to produce materials which are equivalent to that of professional materials developers any more than they are expected to produce sonnets of literary quality in a Shakespeare course. The aim of producing materials is primarily to understand something about how they are constructed -- and why.

A second potential large area of application of social dialect information is to dialect interference in reading. To this point, relatively little has been written on the subject and much of it has been collected in J. Baratz and R. Shuy, eds., Teaching Black Children to Read, Washington, CAL, 1969. Teachers should be encouraged to consider problems of dialect interference through phonology, grammar and orthography and they should examine current beginning reading materials to determine how well they adjust to the linguistic features discussed in earlier courses.

With the introduction of these four courses into the pre-service training program we will be considerably closer to training teachers adequately to meet the language problem of poor, minority group children. It is important, however, that these courses be considered central and not optional or peripheral. The subject matter and skills involved in well taught courses of this sort is, without doubt, among the most important training our future teachers will receive. And this is only, at best, minimal. If students can take additional courses from the available offerings in linguistics it will certainly be to their advantage.

Our first aim is to put the training system in perspective so that teachers who teach language arts courses will be trained in language. But it is foolish to think that we can ignore in-service training entirely. Just as education can not afford to choose between compensatory education and educational overhaul, so teacher training can not really make a choice between pre-service and in-service programs.

Suggested In-Service Programs

Obviously, the most useful way to provide the insights and skills necessary for the intelligent handling of language problems of the ghetto child is for currently employed teachers to study the same subjects that the future teachers are given. The usual compromise is to build some kind of summer workshop or institute which condenses and selects from among the ingredients of these courses and pretends that the same ground has been covered. Another package would be to present all four courses during an eight or ten week summer session. Although either of the above approaches is better than most current situations, neither allows for that important ingredient, maturation time. Just as it is absolutely necessary that the four courses described earlier be taken one at a time, so it is imperative that in-service training allow for the acquisition and digestion of each segment before the next one is attempted. At least, I would suggest no less than a two-summer full-time institute. During the first summer, teachers could study both the Nature of Language and Language Variation. During the second summer they could take Fieldwork in the Language of Children and Teaching Standard English. But better would be a year long part-time program in which the courses are taken one at a time. Better still would be a year of released time for teachers to take a battery of courses in linguistics, teaching English to speakers of other languages, and urban anthropology. If such were possible, it would be wise to expand their course work in the Nature of Language in

order to increase linguistic knowledge and skills. If possible it would also be useful to prepare these teachers as
specialists in English as a second language, especially for
Spanish speakers.

Once the subject matter for such a program is resolved,
an equally important question remains: what agents should
carry out the overhaul required in teacher training if we are
to accomplish the ends set out in the preceding pages? As a
linguist, I would like to think that linguistics departments
would be concerned enough to cooperate with teacher training
programs, even at the expense of becoming involved with mere
applied linguistics. Like it or not, linguists have the
training which is closest to the needs of the moment and it
seems reasonable that an adequate supply of linguists could
be found to handle these courses at selected major teacher
training institutions. The training of linguists has reached
a stage at which it will become increasingly difficult to
find enough teaching jobs in linguistics departments to handle
the number of recent graduates. Thus, the necessary training
in sociolinguistics which has been outlined here can provide
not only an answer to teacher education but also to the im-
pending glut on the job market in linguistics. The danger, if
linguists handle the courses noted above, is that they will
want to wander off into their specialties and create another
educational elite.

The field of linguistics has been relatively late in
coming to grips with contemporary social issues. The matter
of teacher training as outlined in this paper is the closest
such opportunity the discipline may ever have. It would be
tragic for linguists to pass it by.

NOTES

1. The production of this paper was supported largely by
    funds from The United States Office of Education, Bureau
    of Research, Project No. 9-0357.

2. This research is reported fully in Anne E. Hughes, "An
    Investigation of Some Sociolinguistic Phenomena in the
    Vocabulary, Pronunciation and Grammar of Detroit Pre-
    School Children, their Parents and Teachers," Unpublished
    Ed.D. Dissertation, Michigan State University, 1967.

3. This is not to say that such courses do not exist. At
    the time of this writing, several rather comprehensive
    courses of this type are being taught at various American
    universities including UCLA, Columbia Teachers College,
    Georgetown University, Trinity College (D.C.), and North-
    eastern Illinois.

4. See Shuy, "Language Variation and Literacy," in a forth-
    coming IRA publication. See also Joan C. Baratz, in
    this volume, pp. 20-40.

5. For an example of a typescript of this sort, see R. Shuy,
    W. Wolfram and W. Riley, Field Techniques In An Urban
    Language Study, pp. 67-114.

BIBLIOGRAPHY

Baratz, Joan C. and Roger W. Shuy (eds.) Teaching Black
    Children To Read. Washington, D.C.: Center for Applied
    Linguistics, 1969.

Feigenbaum, Irwin. English Now. New York: New Century, 1970.

Gleason, H.A. An Introduction to Descriptive Linguistics.
    Rev. ed. New York: Holt, Rinehart & Winston, 1961.

Golden, Ruth. "Instructional Record for Changing Regional
    Speech Patterns" Folkway/Scholastic, No. 9323.

Hurst, Charles. Psychological Correlates In Dialectolalia.
    Washington, D.C., Howard University, 1965.

Jesperson, Otto. Mankind, Nation and Individual from a
    Linguistic Point of View. Bloomington, Ind.: Indiana
    University Press, 1946.

Labov, William. "Stages in the Acquisition of Standard Eng-
    lish," in R. Shuy (ed.) Social Dialects and Language
    Learning. Champaign, Ill., National Council of Teachers
    of English, 1965.

Lado, Robert. Language Teaching: A Scientific Approach. New York: McGraw-Hill, 1964.

Lin, San-Su. Pattern Practice in the Teaching of Standard English to Students with a Non-Standard Dialect. New York: Columbia University, 1965.

Ray, Punya Sloka. "Language Standardization" in Frank A. Rice (ed.) Study of the Role of Second Languages in Asia, Africa and Latin America. Washington, D.C.: Center for Applied Linguistics, 1962.

Rivers, Wilga M. Teaching Foreign Language Skills. Chicago: University of Chicago Press, 1969.

Shuy, Roger W., Walter A. Wolfram and William K. Riley. Field Techniques in an Urban Language Study, Washington, D.C., Center for Applied Linguistics, 1968.

Slobin, Dan (ed.) A Field Manual for Cross Cultural Study of the Acquisition of Communicative Competence. Berkeley: University of California, 1967.